Bubblecars and Microcars

Other Titles in the Crowood AutoClassic Series

AC Cobra	Brian Laban
Alfa Romeo Spider	John Tipler
Alfa Romeo Sports Coupés	Graham Robson
Aston Martin DB4, DB5 and DB6	Jonathan Wood
Aston Martin and Lagonda V-Engined Cars	David G Styles
Audi quattro	Laurence Meredith
Austin-Healey 100 & 3000 Series	Graham Robson
BMW 3 Series	James Taylor
BMW 5 Series	James Taylor
BMW 7 Series	Graham Robson
BMW M Series	Alan Henry
BMW: The Classic Cars of the 1960s and 70s	Laurence Meredith
Citroën 2CV	Matt White
Citroën DS	Jon Pressnell
Datsun Z Series	David G Styles
Ferrari Dino	Anthony Curtis
Ford RS Escorts	Graham Robson
Jaguar E-Type	Jonathan Wood
Jaguar Mk 1 and 2	James Taylor
Jaguar XJ Series	Graham Robson
Jaguar XJ-S	Graham Robson
Jaguar XK Series	Jeremy Boyce
Jeep – From Bantam to Wrangler	Bill Munro
Lamborghini Countach	Peter Dron
Lotus and Caterham Seven: Racers for the Road	John Tipler
Lotus Elan	Mike Taylor
Lotus Elise	John Tipler
Lotus Esprit	Jeremy Walton
MGA	David G Styles
MGB	Brian Laban
MG T-Series	Graham Robson
Mini	James Ruppert
Morris Minor	Ray Newell
Porsche 911	David Vivian
Porsche 924, 928, 944 and 968	David Vivian
Range Rover	James Taylor and Nick Dimbleby
Rolls-Royce Silver Cloud	Graham Robson
Rolls-Royce Silver Shadow	Graham Robson
Rover P4	James Taylor
Rover P5 & P5B	James Taylor
Rover SD1	Karen Pender
Saab 99 and 900	Lance Cole
Sunbeam Alpine and Tiger	Graham Robson
Triumph 2000 and 2.5PI	Graham Robson
Triumph Spitfire & GT6	James Taylor
Triumph TRs	Graham Robson
TVR	John Tipler
VW Beetle	Robert Davies
Volvo 1800	David G Styles

BUBBLECARS AND MICROCARS

MALCOLM BOBBITT

The Crowood Press

First published in 2003 by
The Crowood Press Ltd
Ramsbury, Marlborough
Wiltshire SN8 2HR

www.crowood.com

British Library Cataloguing-in-Publication Data
A catalogue record for this book is available from the British Library.

ISBN 1 86126 567 0

Acknowledgements
I would like to thank the following people and organizations for their
encouragement and patience in assisting me with this book: Gordon Fitzgerald
who allowed me access to his photographic records and who filled in some of
the background information; Graham Hull for his help regarding
Messerschmitts; BMW GmbH; Reliant Cars; Margaret Ridge; Douglas
Ferreira OBE in respect of his knowledge of Bond Minicars; Frank Delaney;
Volkswagen; Andrew Minney; Martin Bourne; Subaru Cars; H. John Black;
Muriel Cuppage; Metropolitan Police; MCC Smart GmbH; Malcolm Parsons,
Malcolm Thorne, Tom Wood and Jonathon Day at the National Motor
Museum Library; W. R. Faulkner; Ivana Birkettova, Tony Spillane, Roger
Bentley, Lee Turnham, Dave Watson, Paul Robinson, Barrie Allen, Bob
Purton, and Allan Baker of the Quainton Railway Society and, not least, those
owners of various bubblecars and microcars that I photographed. Finally, as
always, my thanks extend to my long-suffering wife Jean who is quite used to
all things motor cars dominating her life.

Unless otherwise credited, all photographs are from the author's collection.

Typeset by Servis Filmsetting Ltd, Manchester

Contents

A trio of Trojans at a microcar event.

Introduction

Bubblecars and microcars are a rare breed. Certain always to attract attention, they are the symbol of a much revered bygone era of motoring history. When I was asked to write this book I viewed the subject with nostalgia and affection. Perceiving it as being an account of those wonderfully eclectic and often idiosyncratic machines such as the Isetta, Heinkel and Messerschmitt, together with the fragile-looking Bond and Reliant, I also came upon the Scootacar, Peel, Gordon, Frisky, Fairthorpe and Goggomobil, to name but a few familiar and not so familiar names. I soon discovered that the world of minimal motoring was far larger and vastly more intriguing than I had thought to be possible.

Being of a certain age, I grew up during the period of post-World War II austerity that engendered the profusion of innovative ultra-economical minicars that were inexpensive to build and run while utilizing the few raw materials that were available. In those days it was unusual to buy anything that wasn't British or Empire made, and what was happening in Europe and beyond seemed hardly to matter. Foreign markets were of course experiencing similar economic difficulties to those of Britain, and there emerged, in terms of motoring, a fascinating collection of vehicles that typified frugality in the extreme.

In researching the advent of the bubblecar and microcar era, I quickly came to accept that the period spanning the late 1940s through to the early 1960s was not the only occasion when motorists had sought alternative forms of independent transportation. The quest for inexpensive personal transport arrived with the coming of the motor car itself, which at first was mainly the domain of the wealthy and aristocracy.

Cyclecars gave way to a variety of austerity machines during the 1920s and 1930s to produce some remarkable examples of innovative engineering. We must not forget that even the Metropolitan Police used BSA three-wheelers to patrol the streets of London during the early 1930s. In an earlier period of history the capital's Bobbies were even seen at work driving the Léon Bollée, now viewed as a machine of great fortitude.

Bubblecars and the like hold a particular sentiment. They recall an era when, despite the Suez crisis and petrol rationing, motorists got on with life against all the odds. These gallant machines afforded only basic comfort and long journeys were something to endure. In the case of the minute Messerschmitt, which allowed motoring for two sitting in tandem beneath a transparent canopy, the term 'people in aspic' was summoned.

Today we see a resurgence of the economy car concept. The fuel crisis of the 1970s and subsequent rising fuel prices, along with growing traffic congestion, have seen to that. Modern microcars have become socially acceptable to the point that they now attract cult following. Fun to look at, pleasing to drive and comparatively inexpensive to run, the microcar is enjoying its renaissance.

Will the new generation of microcars evoke the same sense of pioneering and achievement as did cyclecars and those brave designs that emerged in the wake of World War II? That is a matter of personal opinion.

Malcolm Bobbitt
Cumbria, 2002

A Rytecraft Scootacar. The small size of the car can be ascertained from the size of the driver and the registration plate relative to the size of the car.

1 The Search for Minimal Motoring

The bubblecar and minicar era evolved during the period when post-war austerity and the onset of the Suez crisis created a demand for the cheapest possible motoring. To have a car at all was, at that time, a luxury. There were those who clamoured for anything motorized on wheels as long as it provided a means of independent transportation. A similar situation had occurred previously after World War I – definitely a luxury before 1914, the motor car had been liberated by war, being no longer viewed as the preserve of a fortunate few. The mother of invention came to the fore again in the 1930s when the Great Depression cast its shadow and many motorists looked towards those relatively simple, but no less innovative machines known as cyclecars.

It could be argued that the quest for substantially less expensive motor cars in fact began during elite days of the dawn of motoring. One of the first ventures into minimal motoring arrived with the introduction in 1895 of the Léon Bollée, named after its inventor. This somewhat odd vehicle was blessed with some pretty tricky handling characteristics that made even the most austere of post World War II minicars appear romantic and sophisticated.

As well as being made in France, the 650cc Léon Bollée was built under licence in Coventry at the Motor Mills, an intrinsic part of the Lawson empire. Harry Lawson had planned to dominate British motor manufacturing, but ultimately failed so to do; as for the Léon Bollée, it was to Humber that production had originally been entrusted, that is until Humber's premises were gutted in a disastrous fire in July 1896. The prototype Bollée was destroyed in the inferno, and another vehicle, along with drawings, had to be acquired from Bollée's Le

Mans factory. Then Charles Turrell, Harry Lawson's private secretary, resigned his position with Lawson in order to start car manufacture of his own at the Parkside works in Coventry. It was there that Turrell began making the little Bollée which, by this time, had been given the name the Coventry Motette. Meanwhile, in its rebuilt works, Humber introduced some variations on the Bollée theme, a 'Three-Wheel' Motor Carriage and the Motor Sociable. The former afforded transportation for three, two side by side, with a 'driver' behind sitting on what was essentially a bicycle saddle. The latter was indeed all the more sociable with driver and passenger sitting abreast.

Harry Lawson 1852–1925

Having an engineering background, Harry Lawson became synonymous with the bicycle industry as a designer rather than a manufacturer. He was responsible for the establishment of Rudge Cycles and later was associated with other bicycle manufacturers before turning his attention to motor cars. Lawson believed that he could control the fledgling British motor industry and helped to form the British Motor Syndicate Ltd with capital of £150,000. He also took an option on the Coventry Cotton Mills, which he subsequently renamed the Motor Mills, where, for a time, Humbers were built.

A wealthy entrepreneur, Lawson inspired the formation of the Motor Car Club and floated the Great Horseless Carriage Co. with a capital of £750,000. He was also associated with some rather dubious schemes, however, which left him comparatively penniless when he died, leaving only £99. He is best remembered for organizing the first London to Brighton run to commemorate the passing of the Locomotives on Highways Act of 1896.

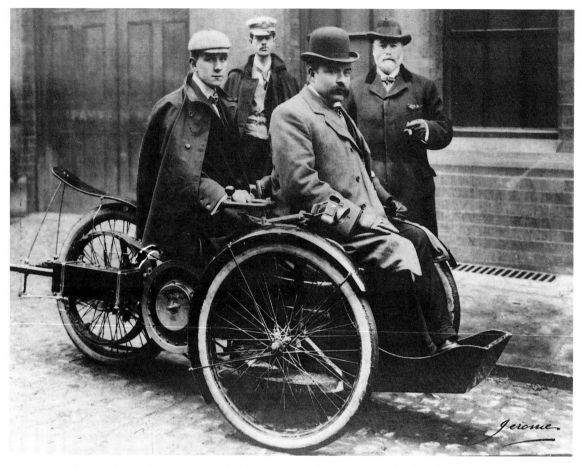

Introduced in 1895, the Léon Bollée was subsequently built at Coventry. At the time it afforded relatively simple and inexpensive motoring despite having some uncertain handling characteristics. (National Motor Museum)

For those intrepid motorists sufficiently brave to endure the Motette – the name being no doubt derived from the French *voiturette*, a term coined by Léon Bollée – certain skills had to be mastered. Difficult to start and keep running, it was, nevertheless, surprisingly fast. Speeds in excess of 30mph (48km/h) were possible under the right conditions, which was nearly double that of some other cars. With the passenger somewhat exposed and seated in a basket ahead of the driver, it was the latter's responsibility to keep the machine on the road. Steering was of the Ackerman type and effected by a small hand wheel on the driver's right. On wet surfaces it was known for the machine to skid in all directions.

What constitutes the little Bollée tandem as being the early forerunner of the minicar is the car's mechanical layout, with the air-cooled 3hp engine being positioned horizontally on the left-hand side of the frame. There was no clutch as such between the engine, with its long shaft, and the gearbox, the crank and flywheel being at opposite ends. Speed-change pinions were located on the engine crankshaft and these were in constant mesh with the gear wheels; to change gear a long 'key' arrangement was positioned to the driver's left, and by twisting it the appropriate gear was selected. The gear lever also acted as one of two slowing devices, for when it was pulled rearwards it allowed the final drive belt rim on the rear wheel to come into contact with a wooden brake block. The second device was in the form of a pedal that activated a brake band directly on the flyweel. A flat leather belt constituted the final drive, which was connected to a pulley on the second motion shaft and the aforementioned rim on the back wheel.

Not only did the Léon Bollée perform extremely well in the first London to Brighton run in 1896, it took the first two places in the time trial between the capital and the south coast. The two Bollées arrived at Brighton within what was then a remarkable time, completing the journey in a fraction over 3 hours and 44 minutes at fastest, and 20 seconds over 4 hours for the other. This is in comparison with 5 hours and 1 minute – the fastest time of the remaining vehicles – and well in excess of 6 hours for the slowest.

That the Bollée tricar out-performed its rivals on that famous run down the Brighton Road at least established the emergence of a plethora of designs that championed motoring for the least amount of money. These were lightly built machines, said by one eminent motorist to be made out of old tin boxes which gave plenty of practice in soldering. Some of the other machines entered for the race were equally as bizarre, such as Sherrin's Electric Bath-Chair and Pennington's tricycle, of which only a handful were made and which were reportedly most unpleasant to ride.

It is not surprising that tricars and quadricycles found a measure of popularity during the late 1890s and early 1900s. A new-found independence was sought by those who could not afford a motor car of 'proper' status. Even so, such customers still generally materialized from the middle classes, businessmen and the professional types who tended to be more affluent. Take Henry Royce, for example. Too much work had made him ill, and his doctor advised him to take up a hobby as a means of relaxation. It was a quadricycle that Royce chose to take him away from his endeavours at Cooke Street in Manchester, and it was that same infernal machine, not an easy contraption to stop once it was going, that more than once landed the engineer into the

cabbage patch in the garden of his Knutsford home.

Whilst the more prosperous in society chose those machines as developed by Daimler, Benz, Lanchester, Panhard, Peugeot and Renault to name but a few marques, others were influenced more by the cycle and motorcycle. Some firms, such as Riley and AC, survived the birth pangs of the motor industry, the former disappearing into oblivion in the 1970s whilst the latter has endured all the ravages that both engineering progress and evolution have provided. There were a number of less familiar names at the time such as Ariel, Beeston, Butler, Swift and Werner, all of which were far more akin to two-wheeled vehicles rather than three or four.

Popular at the time were dog-carts that were often more sophisticatedly referred to as forecars. Whatever the terminology, they were glorified motorbicycles; the driver would sit in the normal position as that of a pedal cycle, handlebars with which to steer, with the passenger ensconced in a basket-type seat ahead, supported by the two front wheels. From smithies where horses were shod, there evolved workshops diversifying into bicycle-making and subsequent repairs, and from these workshops motorcycles, forecars and motor cars were also built and sold.

Motorcycle technology has played a significant role in the development of the cyclecar, the true ancestor of the bubblecar and minicar. Even during those heady formative days of the motor industry it is easy to understand how the metamorphosis from the bicycle to the motorcycle came about. Muscle power conceded to the efficiency of the petrol engine, and relative discomfort gave way to something arguably more agreeable.

The motorized three-wheeler had its beginnings in the 1880s when Edward Butler designed his tricycle, an ingenious affair with a two-stroke twin-cylinder engine connected directly to the single rear wheel. Along with other devices introduced at around the same time, the Butler achieved some notoriety, despite being short-lived and over-shadowed by the compact and relatively simple De Dion-Bouton.

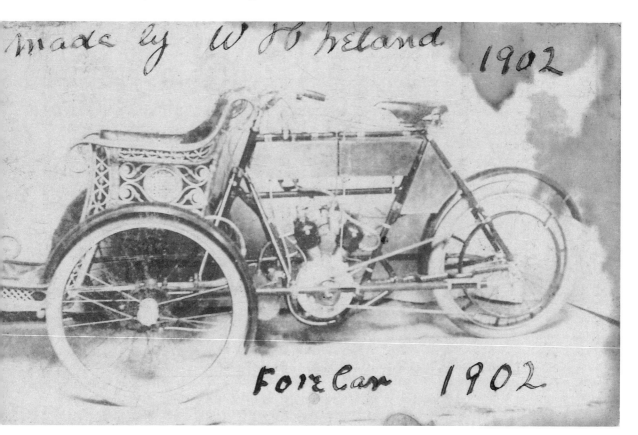

Forecars such as this were popular during the early days of motoring. The Walton, which was built from 1902 by William Ireland of Sankey in Cheshire, a highly respected bicycle manufacture of the period, was just one of a plethora of machines that were available. (Muriel Cuppage)

The harmonization between the Comte Albert De Dion and the very capable Georges Bouton not only brought about some highly sophisticated steam and petrol vehicles, but also a manoeuvrable and easily handled motor tricycle that became an industry standard of the time. The De Dion engine, which was light as well as practical, was used for countless applications; its design was also widely copied. The machine first came into prominence during the 1,062-mile (1,708km) Paris–Marseilles race of 1896. Five De Dion-Bouton tricycles had entered the race, three of which finished the course, and the fastest of these was placed overall third out of a field of thirty-two with an average speed of 14.9mph (24km/h).

Ownership of De Dion-Bouton tricycles had, within a year, become fashionable in Paris, and it was not long before the machine's popularity had spread throughout France and across its borders. Inexpensive to buy and cheap to run, the De Dion-Bouton could be easily handled and, because it was without clutch and gears, required little in the way of technical know-how to keep it going. Having sufficient power to propel it along the flat, the $\frac{3}{4}$bhp engine did require some additional pedal power when starting, and as an aid to climbing hills. (The same applied, many years later with that typically French institution the VeloSolex, and elsewhere with the arrival of the moped.) The assistance of pedal power was quickly made redundant with the introduction of more powerful engines; firstly 1bhp, then $1\frac{1}{4}$bhp, $1\frac{3}{4}$bhp and $2\frac{1}{4}$bhp. The latter became the most popular, albeit for those wanting the ultimate power there was a $2\frac{3}{4}$bhp. Racing machines were also made, and engine sizes up to a maximum of 7bhp were available. Controls were simple – an ignition switch was incorporated in one of the handlebars, and a detachable plug in the handlebar acted as an immobilizer. To increase the machine's speed the carburettor was fitted with a throttle, although generally the practice was to advance the spark.

Forecars to Cyclecars

By the early 1900s the forecar had had its day. A glance through *The Motor* for 1905 depicts a scene whereby the Edwardian motorcar had become firmly established, and the King had taken delivery of a Siddeley car. During August that year the Herkomer Trophy had attracted competitors from Britain who, having had their cars shipped to Boulogne, drove to Munich, which was then a journey of adventurous proportions. The four-seater Rover 16–20bhp had also made its appearance, the 10bhp Ford found a measure of popularity, as did the Vauxhall range of motors. At the opposite spectrum of the motor market the Phoenix Trimo attracted some attention when the $4\frac{1}{4}$bhp Minerva-engined cyclecar completed a trial between Liverpool and Kilmarnock, the distance of 217 miles (350km) being completed in 13 hours. Much was made of the fact that the vehicle managed to climb the redoubtable Shap Fell (now the highest point on the M6 motorway) with driver and passenger up.

As motor cars became all the more sophisticated in design, equipment and comfort, so the gulf between luxury cars and the more minimal types widened. The four-cylinder, two-seater Leader was one of the smaller motor cars of the time and was priced at 200 guineas, whilst the Gregoire Light Car sold for £165. American cars attracted some popularity too, and the little two-seater, twin-cylinder 7bhp Pope Tribune was offered for 125 guineas.

Several types of light car of a basic design were marketed to a clientele who were happy to sacrifice sophisticated engineering for independence and economy, even if it meant enduring a certain

lack of comfort. Chater-Lea, better known for its motorcycles, was one such utility vehicle, the chain-driven rear wheels being powered by a 6bhp V-twin engine mounted on the off side of the frame. For customers content with such frugality there was ample choice of machines, but for those requiring the most simple and basic affairs, American machines known as buckboards could be acquired for under £100. The penalty for such thriftiness was having to tolerate tiller steering and the absence of any springing or coachwork. Having equally uncomplicated engineering, buckboards more often than not had feeble engines directly driving the rear axle, thus permitting only a single speed.

A new direction in ultra-light car design emerged with machines, both three- and four-wheelers, which employed front-wheel drive. The idea had been simple enough in the beginning, Harry Lawson having introduced the Motor Wheel that incorporated engine, fuel tank, brake and steering device. The notion had been that the Motor Wheel could be attached to any type of vehicle that was, essentially, designed to be horse-driven. It was not long before uncomplicated two-wheel bodies became available to which the Motor Wheel could be connected. Purpose-built trikes rapidly found a market, and the concept could again be found decades later in the form of the Bond Minicar. Four-wheel front-drivers were all the more complicated, despite employing some engineering crudity; when one such design, the Victoria Combination, was entered into trials events, the resulting enthusiasm led to the sale of some 400 machines.

The cyclecar era was at its height from the turn of the century to the onset of World War I. Particular types of machine were identified as being cyclecars, a term which had been coined by *The Motor Trader* in 1912 to describe a vehicle that was more substantial than a motorcycle, while falling short of being a *real* car. Cyclecars owed their evolution to the motorcycle and sidecar combination, which, at least, afforded some measure of social transportation for the small family. From modest beginnings there proliferated a series of designs, all of which indicated that a powerful lobby of 'new motorists' was emerging, influenced, no doubt as far as Britain was concerned, by the fact that it had a greater number of cars on the road than any neighbouring European country. That is not an indicator that Britain's motor industry was the keenest at the time; in fact, it was France which was leading production, with Britain lagging well behind in second place, and Germany and Italy taking third and fourth positions respectively.

Despite its relatively crude and unsophisticated design, the cyclecar was, nevertheless, capable of substantial performance. Long journeys were certainly within the ability of such machines, and improving technology meant that components such as engines, gearboxes, carburettors, ignition systems and tyres were all the more reliable. As more refinements became available, such as electric lighting and starting, so the cyclecar was eventually equipped according to price and specification.

Increasing levels of interest in cyclecars led to the formation of the Cyclecar Club on 30 October 1912, the first meeting being convened at the Holborn Restaurant in London. Its first driving event was held on 7 December 1912, when a run from London to the Wisley Hut Hotel near Esher was arranged. *The Cyclecar* magazine was also first published in 1912, and its appearance was certainly instrumental in promoting the cyclecar movement in Britain. Within a few months, the journal's name was changed to *The Light Car & Cyclecar*, and remained as such until 1933 when it became known as *The Light Car* until the publication's demise in December 1956. Cyclecar clubs were formed elsewhere, not least France where Le Cyclecar Club de France was established, and subsequently a number of dedicated journals were promoted both in Europe and America.

The proliferation of cyclecars quickly exposed the fact that many machines were capable of outperforming cars costing considerably more. There is little surprise that owners and enthusiasts of cyclecars were soon viewed with some hostility by other motorists, and, as it transpired,

by motorcyclists. The Auto-Cycle Union, sensing a potential loss of income by discouraging cyclecar owners from joining its ranks, quickly found itself at odds with established motorcyclists. The solution was to seek a definition that allowed cyclecars to stand alone in their own right.

Among the first cyclecars was the Bédélia, created in France by Robert Bourbeau in 1910. Bourbeau was eighteen years old when he designed the Bédélia, the forerunner of machines built in a small factory in Paris. It had a remarkable sales record despite its peculiar design. It was designed as a four-wheel, two-seater tandem, the passenger sitting ahead of the driver in forecar practice. Powered by a motorcycle engine positioned immediately aft of the front wheels, drive was effected via a two-speed belt arrangement connecting with the rear wheels. Steering and springing were equally simple – a cable and bobbin attached to a centre pivot front axle allowed the entire assembly to turn, and a centrally mounted coil spring provided the means of front suspension. Even more anomalous was the fact that the vehicle could not be driven without a passenger, whose task it was to change gear by means of moving the drive belts from one pulley to another using a stick.

Driving a Bédélia fitted with a 10bhp V-twin engine, Bourbeau entered the 1913 Cyclecar Grand Prix at Amiens, which he won. His success at the event no doubt influenced sales, one of the first cars being supplied to a doctor. Nick Georgano reveals in *The Beaulieu Encyclopaedia of the Automobile* that the doctor used his Bédélia as an ambulance, raising questions as to how the patient coped with changing gear! Advancing technology meant that during World War I Bédélias were equipped with the means to allow the driver to change gear.

The growing popularity of the cyclecar meant that a whole new industry surrounding what was known as 'new motoring' (translated more correctly as *minimal motoring*) was rapidly developing. No more than a dozen cyclecar manufacturers in Britain, with a commensurate number in France, were listed in 1911, and yet by 1914 those figures

In spite of its eccentricities, the Bédélia found many customers. Dating from 1910, this tandem had the driver sitting behind the passenger, whose task it was to change gear using a stick! Judging from the Belgian-registered vehicles in the background, and the girl's attire, the photograph dates from the 1950s. (National Motor Museum)

had multiplied tenfold. The same situation occurred in Germany and Austria as well as other European countries.

A subsequent move to export the cyclecar theme to the United States failed, mainly because fuel there was cheap and abundantly available. Instead, America developed a love affair with the Model T Ford and other full-size motor cars that were inexpensive to produce and which found a willing market. Despite this, a small number of cyclecars were built in the US, among which the Imp was popular. It was built by W.H. McIntyre, a manufacturer of full-size cars.

Two particular makes associated in Britain with the early cyclecar era are GN and Morgan. The former was the product of H.R. Godfrey and Archie Frazer-Nash, both of whom were young engineers working at Willans and Robinson at Rugby. It was at the works at Rugby where the engineers, still in their teens, built their first car. Apart from some minor fittings all the components were acquired from the works except the

magneto and engine; the former was a Bosch item, the latter a V-twin JAP or Peugeot.

There was more than an element of success awaiting the two engineers. Production of the little GN was transferred to Frazer-Nash's home in Golders Green Road, Hendon, where the stables accommodated the workshop. Six cars were built there before the premises' limitations meant that a move to a larger building was necessary. A series of sheds occupied by several small businesses at The Burroughs, elsewhere in Hendon, provided suitable quarters. It was there that the fledgling business expanded; Godfrey and Frazer-Nash built their own V-twin engines using Peugeot cylinders and valves along with inlet over exhaust cylinder heads engineered to their design.

The GN achieved a considerable reputation through its performance. Of only 12bhp, it nevertheless had a top speed of around 60mph (97km/h), the engine being positioned transversely in a lightweight ash frame. A two-speed chain and dog clutch formed part of the

The GN was the forerunner of the Frazer-Nash and was one of the most respected cyclecars. Early examples were built in a workshop at Archie Frazer-Nash's home before production was transferred to The Burroughs in Hendon. (National Motor Museum)

transmission system, the final drive being effected by belts. Further design development included modified engines and new models, and by the outbreak of war in 1914, the GN was recognized as being among the best cyclecars then available. In 1919 GN was sold to the British Gregoire Co., after which the initial design was substantially modified. In the same year the French Salmson company bought a licence to produce the GN in France, an arrangement that lasted for three years. Under new ownership, sales of GN cars increased significantly, but the boom was short lived. In early post-war years sales slumped; a receiver was appointed in 1922 and the company was sold, the new owner choosing to enter the touring car market.

The other popular cyclecar was the Morgan, a name that is ironically epitomized nowadays by elite sports cars. There is, nevertheless, a loyal and enthusiastic following for three-wheeled Morgans, on which the company built its reputation. The company was established during the formative days of the cyclecar, era when H.F.S. Morgan built his Morgan Runabout in 1909. As a single-seater it failed to attract much attention when displayed at the Motor Cycle Show at Olympia in 1910. Motorists were more interested in two-seater machines, and Morgan therefore offered a suitable machine at the 1911 Motor Cycle Show. During the months between the two shows Morgan had competed in a number of sporting events and achieved particular recognition, so much so that by the end of the 1911 exhibition Morgan's order books were full.

Morgan – The Early Years

The Morgan Motor Company is unique in that it has survived as an independent car maker since its establishment in 1912. Also unique is the fact that today the company is still run by the Morgan family. The Morgan Motor Car, soon to become the archetypal three-wheeler, survived most other sporting trikes, and today its design, build and performance are legendary. H.F.S. Morgan was born on 11 August 1881 in the Malvern Hills, the son of a vicar. While growing up, he formed a particular attachment to cars and, having attended the Crystal Palace Engineering College, designed and built his own bicycle.

Later, when he returned to Herefordshire, H.F.S. was so impressed with motorcycles and motor cars that he hired a number of machines from Marriot's motor business in Hereford, the first in the county. When it came to purchasing a motor vehicle of his own, H.F.S. chose an Eagle tandem tricar. He then decided to start his own motor business, which he did from his home on Worcester Road, Malvern Link. The Morgan factory today may be far removed from the company's humble beginnings, but the name will be forever linked with the first Morgan Runabout.

JAP-engined Aero Morgans were a familiar sight for many years. This recently photographed example dates from the early 1930s; to the left can be seen an F-Type, the last of the three-wheelers.

Similarly to the GN, the first Morgans had V-twin engines with Peugeot barrels, and transmission was courtesy of dog clutches and chain drives. A changeover to JAP engines was made, and in 1912 a Morgan set a new cyclecar record when it covered 58.96 miles (94.8km) in an hour at Brooklands. The prototype Morgan was built in the engineering workshop of Malvern College, and in 1910 the Morgan Motor Co. was established in Malvern Link with capital that H.F.S. Morgan had acquired from his father. Additional workshop space was attained in 1919 at Pickersleigh Road, Malvern Link, the home of the company today.

A host of fragile-looking cyclecars emerged in the period just before World War I. Some, like the south-west London-built La Rapide, appeared little more than a child's toy; others, such as the Yorkshire-built JBS, were the precursors to much more substantial light cars. In France and Germany there was a similar position, and in the case of the former, simplicity was the order of the day. The French, having a penchant for engineering that appeared crude but nevertheless was logical and mostly reliable, were able to put together all sorts of weird contraptions that could be easily repaired by any *garagiste*. The onset of war changed the course of automotive history, and the days of the cyclecar were numbered.

The Twenties and Post-War Austerity

World War I put the motor vehicle firmly on the map. For the first time in hostilities the motor car was the motive force, not the horse. Consequently, motor vehicles became a way of life for many more people than had been the case before 1914, and a demand for them was, during the immediate post-war period, quickly established in what was a period of financial boom.

When boom rapidly turned to decline it was the makers of luxury cars that mainly felt the chill of austerity. Thus we see such prestigious companies as Rolls-Royce keen to introduce smaller and less expensive cars, albeit still firmly in the luxury league. As quickly as a myriad of manufacturers of averagely priced motors proliferated,

so the depression ensured that they went out of business. However, for the manufacturers of cyclecars and even lesser types of vehicle there appeared to be no shortage of buyers. Companies profited by trading on the gratuities that were paid to service personnel, some of whom nevertheless decided that a light car, rather than a cyclecar, was the better proposition.

Whilst a number of cyclecars were relatively sophisticated, some of the designs that emerged during the shadow of war were decidedly Heath–Robinson. Rudimentary plywood bodies remained sufficient for some car makers, along with simple air-cooled motorcycle engines and belt drive. As customers became all the more discerning, manufacturers complied with demand. Belt drives were superseded by chain drives, cable and bobbin steering eventually gave way to somewhat more sophisticated geometry.

Among some of the more notable designs of austerity vehicles was the Carden, a product of a prolific inventor who was interested in both the motor car and the aeroplane. Pre-war, John Valentine Carden had built monocars, and post-war he developed his design as a side-by-side two-seater, originally costing £100. It was a rear-engined machine with a horizontal twin two-stroke engine with its cylinders positioned alongside each other rather than horizontally opposed and the rear axle was driven via a two-speed gearbox. Carden sold the firm in 1921, and the new owners, Arnott & Harrison, brought out a new model, which they called the New Carden. They increased the price without any substantial mechanical improvement to the model, with the result that for only a few pounds more a proper light car could be afforded.

Tamplins of south-west London, known in more recent years as motor-car agents, were once agents for the Carden JAP-engined V-twin 8bhp monocar and two-seater models. Having bought the rights to the model from John Carden, some 2,000 machines were sold as the Tamplin and were recognized for their unique design.

That Carden was also involved in aircraft design is significant. As in the post World War II era, a number of aircraft manufacturers turned to cyclecar building as a means of diversifying their trade. A.V. Roe, Graham–White and Armstrong-Siddeley were among those aeroplane and aero engine makers that were tempted to motor car building. It seems unlikely that any Avro cars were actually sold, although there is evidence that at least one prototype cyclecar existed. The company was more attracted towards light cars and again there is evidence that the Ford Model T engine was specified. The pioneer aviator Claude Graham–White produced three models of cyclecar, a buckboard which relied only on the flexing of the frame as a means of suspension, and the wholly more substantial 7HP and Wonder Car. The latter machines were basic enough, the Wonder Car having a 348cc 3.5bhp precision engine and a two-speed gearbox; the 7HP was virtually identical except for its 685cc Coventry Victor flat-twin engine and friction transmission.

Armstrong-Siddeley's venture into cyclecar making materialized with the Stoneleigh, of which several hundred were built. One of the features of the car was that the driver sat centrally in the cabin with the two passenger seats positioned slightly aft. A van version was also built, a number of which were sold to the Royal Mail. The role of aircraft manufacturers diversifying into cyclecar making did not perpetuate because the growth of civil aviation soon fully occupied aviation companies.

A JAP-engined Carden cyclecar is being lowered from the first-floor workshop of John Carden's Teddington premises around 1914. (Margaret Ridge)

Carden moved to Ascot in 1919 and produced this two-seater. The 707cc engine with its side-by-side twin cylinders was located at the rear, driving the rear axle through a two-speed gearbox. (National Motor Museum)

In 1919 the Cyclecar Club changed its name to the Junior Car Club. Possibly the club recognized that the cyclecar era, despite what was then a boom period in minimal motoring, would eventually have its day. The Junior Car Club promoted, in the autumn of 1921, a 200-mile race, an event that was staged every year until 1928. The venue was none other than Brooklands and such personalities as Archie Frazer-Nash could be relied upon to provide some entertaining driving. GNs were already performing to exemplary standards, as was illustrated when Rex Munday, under RAC observation, drove from London to Edinburgh without stopping the engine. With such splendid reliability, it is little

wonder that production of GNs was often in excess of fifty a week.

The end of the cyclecar era was now in sight. The margin between the cyclecar and a number of small but more sophisticated machines was rapidly diminishing. For a relatively modest additional investment, customers would soon be able to purchase a motor car such as the Austin Seven. Nevertheless, there remained a market for some out and out utility vehicles that were the epitome of minimal motoring.

The tiny Xtra is a good example of such utility vehicles, being hardly anything more than a motorized sidecar powered by a 269cc Villiers engine. The Co-Operative Wholesale Society

The Stoneleigh was built by Armstrong-Siddeley, a company associated with rather more prestigious cars than this cyclecar. A van was also included in the Stoneleigh catalogue, and a number were used by the Royal Mail. (National Motor Museum)

(Co-Op) was also the producer of a thrifty cyclecar, which, as a three-wheeler, sold for £150. Few cars could boast such unconventionality as A.A. Scott's Sociable; with its single front wheel the tiny four-seater resembled something more akin to a motor scooter. The same could be said of the Harper Runabout, which was even more utilitarian, but which, nevertheless, was a competent competitor in trials events.

The age of the cyclecar was more prolonged on mainland Europe than in Britain, the reason being that both France and Germany in particular suffered more acutely from raw material shortages during the aftermath of war. Thus such machines as the Hanomag and Monotrace found favour among customers along with a series of vehicles that were designed by Marcel Violet, all of which featured a measure of logical engineering that often appeared all the more illogical to British tastes.

Some bizarre designs of miniature cars emerged from Germany during the mid 1920s, no doubt as a result of the dire consequences of the deutschmark's collapse in 1922. Even the most crude affairs attracted customers who were happy to acquire what were essentially motorized prams. The single-seater Slaby Beringer was one such machine which was sold as the SB; having a simple wooden body attached to four wheels without a chassis, the electric motor afforded propulsion of sorts before motorcycle engines were fitted courtesy of DKW. Surprisingly, the electrically powered SB was available in Britain when it was sold through Gamages, London's famous Holborn department store. Other diminutive electric cars emanating from Germany included the Hawa, which owed its origins to railway carriage construction. Many such vehicles were short lived, but a number of firms building them did survive well into the late 1920s.

This happy scene depicts the highly unusual Scott Sociable with its unconventional wheel arrangement. (National Motor Museum)

Despite its diminutive size and utilitarian appearance, the Harper Runabout with its 269cc engine proved itself in competition events. Some 500 examples were sold between 1921 and 1926, and all were made in A.V. Roe's aircraft factory. (National Motor Museum)

Of French machines of the period none were so eccentric as the tandem-seat Leyat, which owed its design to aero engineering. One could be forgiven for thinking that the vehicle was nothing other than a four-wheel aeroplane minus its wings, given that its means of propulsion was a petrol-engine-driven propeller. The French nevertheless did build some sporting three-wheelers that were akin to the British Morgan. D'Yrsan was the maker of one such cyclecar, its fortune being that it could exceed 80mph (130km/h). Morgans were built under licence in France by two companies, Darmont and Sandford.

The Great Depression Takes its Toll

The events of the 1930s were the influencing factors for the emergence of post-war minicars and bubblecars. Again it was the French and Germans who perpetuated frugal motoring. One of the foremost engineers of minicars was Josef Ganz who, being Jewish, was forced to flee Germany and to take refuge in Switzerland in 1937. Ganz was a prolific designer, creating a number of ideas for manufacturers, including Adler. Among the many designs Ganz produced, of which only a very few ever materialized into production, was the Wilhelm Gutbrod-built Standard Superior. This, like most of Ganz's efforts, featured a backbone chassis and a tiny rear-mounted twin-cylinder, two-stroke engine. Of aerodynamic shape, Ganz's car sported a bonnet that sloped sharply at the front following the contours of the wheel arches, and a tail that curved as neatly.

Almost aerodynamic in appearance was Carl Borgward's Goliath Pioneer, a name which was somewhat at odds with the car's diminutive size. Unlike the Gutbrod Standard Superior, the Goliath was a three-wheeler possessing a conventional chassis with a 198cc two-stroke, single-cylinder Ilo engine mounted at the rear.

Few motor vehicles were as idiosyncratic as the Leyat. Driven by an ABC or Anzani engine connected to a propeller, there was no need for a gearbox or, therefore, a transmission system. Early machines had open bodies, but later examples were fitted with an enclosed cabin. (National Motor Museum)

French cyclecar builders produced some particularly sporting machines in the vogue of the Morgan. This is the 8HP D'Yrson. (National Motor Museum)

Carl Borgward 1890–1963

Born in Hamburg in 1890, Carl Borgward trained to be an engineer. When he joined the Bremer Kühler-fabrik tyre factory, after 1919 he put his adroit organizing skills to good use and helped to restructure the company as a manufacturer of mainly three-wheeled utility vehicles. In 1929 Borgward bought a controlling interest in the firm's largest customer, Hansa-Lloyd Werke AG. After World War II, Borgward oversaw the rebuilding of his car factories in record time; all car manufacturing ceased after 1961.

Compared to the car's overall dimensions, the wheels appeared relatively large, which nevertheless gave it a surefooted appearance. A two-seater with hardly sufficient space for two children, the tiny Goliath afforded the most awkward driving position. This was owing to the car's steering wheel being positioned at a steep angle, which was necessary due to the lack of interior space and the angle of the windscreen, which was perpendicular.

The Goliath name began in 1924 when Carl Borgward chose it to front a series of small three-wheeler vans. The Pioneer was introduced in 1931 and such vehicles could be driven without the owner having to pay an annual tax or having to be in possession of a driving licence. This policy was changed after 1933, and therefore ownership of tiny three-wheelers became less attractive.

For out and out frugality, nothing could match Charles Mochet's Velocar, which relied upon nothing more complicated than pedal power. With such low running costs is there any wonder that the contraption sold well? From 1929 onwards, it was offered with mechanical aid in the form of a 142cc engine.

Just as peculiar were the Rytecraft Scootacars and Scootatrucks that made their appearance in 1934 (which had nothing to do with the Scootacar that was introduced in the 1950s by Hunslet Engineering). These really were cars and commercials in miniature, and although some 1,500 examples were sold, they were hardly suitable for serious road use. Their role was mainly one of publicity, although many were used in working situations on private estates and within factory premises.

In addition to the Morgan, which continued to attract a loyal and sporting clientele, a number of other three-wheelers were popular to a degree in Britain, notably the Coventry Victor, BSA and Raleigh. Each of these cars afforded relatively sophisticated motoring compared to some of the more eccentric offerings of the period. Whilst the three mentioned vehicles displayed an element of affinity to the motorcycle and sidecar, they shared a far greater kinship to motor car design and practice.

The Coventry Victor should not be confused with the Coventry Premier, which owed its origins, in part, to William Hillman. During the interwar years Premier introduced a three-wheel cyclecar, but when Singer took over the firm in 1921 the car was phased out in favour of a four-wheeler using the cyclecar's engine and gearbox. Coventry Victor was, until 1911, known as Morton & Weaver, W.A. Weaver being a designer and builder of aeroplanes, one of which, the Ornithoplane, was one of the first mono-planes to take to the skies over Britain.

One of the smallest cars ever built was the Rytecraft Scootacar, this example having been pictured while taking part in the 1969 Calcutta Vintage Rally. (National Motor Museum)

Coventry Victor three-wheelers often attracted the name 'Country Vicar'. Nevertheless, they were popular and frequented sporting events. Early models were fitted with 688cc water-cooled, flat-twin side-valve engines. (National Motor Museum)

Coventry Victor three-wheelers (they attracted the nickname 'Country Vicar') when introduced in 1926 were fitted with the firm's side-valve 688cc flat-twin water-cooled engine, a version of which had been designed for motorcycle use. The same model, known as the Midget, was built for six years, with the majority of examples having two-seater open bodies. A few, however, were supplied with coupé-type bodies courtesy of Avon coachbuilders of Warwick. In 1932 the design of the Coventry Victor underwent a substantial change after C.F. Beauvais had been invited to submit a restyling exercise. Beauvais was successful as a stylist during the interwar period and had built the CFB to his own design, although the car enjoyed only limited sales. He was, however, far more noted for his styling of the Lanchester Ten and the Avon Standards, and his revamping of the Crossley Three Litre. Beauvais' version of the Coventry Victor was marketed as the Luxury Sports and, as such, was equipped with fashionable coachwork that was finished in a two-tone colour scheme. Adding to the package of changes was a 749cc ohv engine and a three-speed gearbox; the model came with a price tag of £110. Before production stopped in 1937, more powerful engines of 850cc, 900cc and, finally,

1,000cc, were offered, although the original design remained available at £75.

The price of three-wheelers during the 1920s and 1930s was the topic of much discussion, especially in light of the fact that the £100 motor car was frequently aired in the motoring press of the era. At the end of the 1920s it was feasible to purchase a good quality three-wheeler that was comprehensively equipped for around £90, a figure in excess of that often being required to purchase many sidecar combinations. Prices of second-hand machines tended to be proportionally higher than relative four-wheelers, the reason being that while the lower tax was obviously an advantage, the simplicity of the vehicles, both mechanically and in construction, made overhauls easier and therefore there was less likelihood of a machine being in a drastically poor condition.

BSA was another forerunner in tricar design during the interwar years. The largest motorcycle builders in Britain, BSA introduced its three-wheeler in 1929. Designed by F.W. Hulse, the car was built at BSA's Small Heath factory and offered an alternative to the Morgan and Coventry Victor. The BSA's engine was a 1,021cc V-twin of Hotchkiss design. The Beeza, as it was affectionately known, had double transverse leaf inde-

BSA

The origins of the Birmingham Small Arms Co. date to around 1700, although the firm was formed as a limited company in 1861. Bicycles were manufactured from 1880 until 1982, although by then this enterprise was owned by Raleigh Industries. BSA became involved with the motor industry around 1900 with the manufacture of automotive components. BSA took over Daimler in 1910, and following World War I began building light cars as well as luxury vehicles. BSA also produced motorcycles from 1910 and within two decades had become the largest supplier of motorcycles in the UK. BSA also built three-wheel cars that attracted a popular following, not only as family vehicles but also as rugged sporting machines. The three-wheelers to some extent rivalled Morgans, and were, unusually for the period, designed with front-wheel drive. BSA car production was not resumed after World War II and instead the name was used to concentrate on the manufacture of motorcycles.

pendent front suspension and front-wheel drive, something that was quite unusual at the time.

Announced at the 1929 Motor Cycle Show, the BSA attracted a good deal of attention. Several models were available, with similar mechanical specifications but differing styles of bodies in various trim formats. The two-seater is the more familiar, although a family version with two small seats at the rear that were suitable for children was available; all models were fitted with all-round weather protection and, unusually for such a car, were equipped with electric starting. The BSA proved itself over many occasions at sporting events, and it was these successes, along with its robustness and price, that resulted in some 2,000 vehicles a year leaving the factory.

Among the more unusual roles performed by BSAs was that of London traffic patrol cars in service with the Metropolitan Police in the early 1930s. The fact they were used for police work is a good indicator of their quality and suitability

Britain's largest motorcycle manufacturer, BSA, produced this elegant three-wheeler from 1929. Affectionately known as Beezas, they were competent machines and were a familiar sight at rally events. Powered by a 1021cc V-twin engine, the BSA featured double transverse leaf independent front suspension and front-wheel drive.

BSAs were used by the Metropolitan Police for traffic duties during the early 1930s. (Metropolitan Police)

for hard work. From 1933 until 1936 a four-cylinder engine of 1,075cc capacity was available, which ultimately was used in the Scout four-wheel model.

The third make of car to enjoy particular success was the Raleigh which, like BSA, emerged from a company specializing in cycles. The company had built the Raleighette tricar in 1903 and, two years later, experimented with a prototype car. Between then and the early 1930s, Raleigh's output comprised two-wheel machines. In 1932 the company made available a single-cylinder 598cc motor tricycle in van form before introducing a passenger-carrying version. The driver sat on a saddle and steered the front wheel with handlebars, the passengers sitting in the rear compartment. The success of this rather odd little vehicle can be judged as being somewhat limited, especially at the price of £89.

Raleigh, the Precursor to Reliant

The following year Raleigh introduced the Safety Seven, a wholly more sophisticated machine, which, despite its single front wheel, shared much with motor car practice. Gone was the single-cylinder engine, in its place a JAP

742cc V-twin along with a three-speed gearbox and shaft drive to the rear axle. The Safety Seven was offered in tourer and saloon versions and was designed by Tom Williams who, before having joined Raleigh, had worked for Triumph designing motorcycles.

The Safety Seven proved itself in competitive events during its short career. In production for fewer than three years, the car sold moderately well with around 1,000 leaving the factory. In 1934 Raleigh decided not to continue three-wheeler development, but production lasted until 1936, after which the company concentrated on making bicycles. For Tom Williams the decision was unpalatable and he left Raleigh intent on promoting and furthering the design of his three-wheeler van, which he named the Reliant.

Tom Williams established the Reliant Engineering Co. in 1935 in a shed in the grounds of his home at Tamworth in Staffordshire, later moving to premises that had been a depot for the Midland Red bus company. Williams designed his three-wheeler around the front assembly of a Raleigh motorcycle, using the single-cylinder, air-cooled engine that had powered the Raleigh motor tricycle. The prototype was no doubt a rather crude affair with its handlebar steering, but

---

Tom Williams 1890–1964

Tom Lawrence Williams is one of the unsung heroes of the British motor industry. Born in 1890, Tom gained an engineering background before taking up an appointment with Triumph, at the age of 25, and later with Dunford & Elliott of Sheffield. In 1929 he joined the Raleigh Cycle Co. in Nottingham where he was responsible for the design of the Raleigh Safety Seven three-wheeled, two-seater economy car. When Raleigh decided to concentrate solely on cycle manufacturing, Williams, believing there to be a future for lightweight three-wheeled utility cars, left Raleigh to establish his own vehicle manufacturing business, Reliant Engineering, the product being the Reliant van and, later, the Reliant motor car. Tom Williams was a gifted engineer whose products became a household name, and which gave affordable transport to many thousands of families.

Having introduced a 598cc motor tricycle van in 1932, Raleigh unveiled the Safety Seven in 1933. This was a sophisticated machine that was powered by a 742cc JAP V-twin engine driving the rear axle via a three-speed gearbox. (National Motor Museum)

development quickly produced a far more sophisticated arrangement with a proper chassis, shaft drive to the rear axle and a steering wheel.

Production of the Reliant began early in 1935 and delivery of the first van was made on 3 March. A number of refinements were made in the wake of experience with early production, but the most significant concerned the engine. Williams negotiated to use the Austin Seven power plant, but this arrangement was short lived because, in 1938, production of the engine was stopped. Overcoming what could have been a desperate situation, Reliant set up its own engine-building plant to produce a unit similar to that of the Austin but featuring some modifications.

The decision to build its own engines meant that Reliant was able to contribute towards the war effort throughout World War II by building components for the War Ministry. Reliant's own engines were produced after the onset of war but were not used for Reliant vehicle production until 1946.

Ending an Era

Production of Morgans continued throughout the 1930s, but even for such a successful company, the winds of change were felt. The Aero model with its twin-rail tube chassis that had performed so well competitively was joined by a more conventional chassis arrangement that was the F-Type. No longer was the engine

Tom Williams anticipated that there would be a market for a three-wheeler that was both economical and soundly constructed. This is a prototype model featuring handlebar steering and chain drive. (National Motor Museum)

The Reliant progressed to a more substantial chassis featuring car-type steering and shaft-driven rear axle. Williams negotiated to use the Austin Seven engine, which is shown here. When Austin stopped producing the engine, Williams designed his own engine, which was built by Reliant. (National Motor Museum)

exposed; indeed, under the bonnet existed a 933cc side-valve four-cylinder Ford unit that could normally be found on the Model Y Ford. For those who wanted a smoother running engine the F-Type performed admirably, but there were those who cast a suspicious eye towards the Malvern company. Introduction of the F-Type signalled a change in production – four-wheelers were becoming the mainstay of Morgan output, and during the period immediately before World War II relatively few three-wheelers were built. Production of the F-Type did continue post-war, but only in small numbers, the last car rolling out of Pickersleigh Road in July 1952.

Minimal motoring in the true sense was in serious decline by the end of the 1930s. Innovation and necessity were not as paramount as they had once been. However, events in Europe were about to dictate serious change once more, which would again be reflected in the world of motoring.

2   In Time of Need 1946–1950

One could be forgiven for thinking that the era of minimal motoring had been left behind in the second part of the 1930s. Certainly there were still light cars, as they were often referred to, but they were generally a far cry from that element of frugality that had once attracted a specific clientele. However, by 1946, World War II had drained the very essence of manufacturing throughout Europe and as far away as Japan. What little steel there was tended to be of poor quality, and as for raw materials generally, there was a dearth. Industry was in tatters and throughout the engineering heartlands there was smouldering devastation.

Keep it Small, Keep it Cheap

With hostilities at an end, countries that had been ravaged by war took stock of their situation. As far as Britain was concerned its automobile manufacturing potential was relatively sound, as long as sufficient quantities of raw materials could be made available. To some extent the shadow factory scheme, which had been introduced in the mid-1930s to prepare the armed services for conflict, was the industry's saviour. Originally built to provide aero engines and aircraft components, shadow factories had been largely administered by the motor industry, and once demand for fighting equipment had diminished, such factories were mainly allotted to vehicle manufacture.

The return to car making in Britain was a painful business. Assembly lines that had been converted to supplying for the war effort were, where it remained possible, transformed to their earlier roles. The hiatus in motor production had left most manufacturers without new designs with which to begin production, and the creation of new ideas took time and stretched resources. Pre-war designs were reinstated as a stopgap while new models were conceived. As a marketing and political move this, in hindsight, proved to be something of a disaster for the British motor industry. Only when car manufacturers had embarked on a course which, again in hindsight, could arguably have been far better orchestrated, did the government of the day specify conditions which meant there being few cars available for the home market.

The government decreed that the limited stocks of raw materials should be reserved for a massive export drive, with the result that the average British motorist was starved of independent means of transport. In times of austerity there was the additional factor that many would-be motorists simply could not afford to buy the motor car of their choice, even had it been readily available. Waiting lists for new cars indicated that delivery times were very extended. Petrol rationing, which had been introduced in the United Kingdom on 16 July 1939, continued until 26 May 1950.

Petrol rationing was reintroduced during the Suez crisis and remained in force from December 1956 to May 1957. Sufficient fuel for approximately 200 miles (320km) per month was allowed, and in some cases the allocation was significantly less. The more economical cars were obviously beneficial to motorists.

The aftermath of war and its social and political consequences resulted in the emergence of a proliferation of tiny cars that were designed both to be economical to construct as well as to use.

Petrol Rationing

Petrol rationing was administrated to afford motor-cyclists 2 gallons (9ltr) a month, and owners of cars up to 7bhp were allowed 4 gallons (18ltr) a month. Larger engined cars, of 8 and 9bhp, were allotted 5 gallons (23ltr) monthly, and so the scale continued to a maximum of 10 gallons (46ltr) for 20bhp vehicles. All petrol was pooled but it consisted of two types, clear for domestic use and pink for military and commercial consumption. Pink petrol was available in vastly more generous quantities than the clear variety, and it goes without saying that there existed a number of profiteers supplying 'black market' pink fuel to general motorists. Certain exemptions to rationing were made, and doctors, farmers and other 'essential' users received allowances well above those afforded to other car owners.

Shortages of raw materials sometimes also resulted in the use of unconventional means of construction together with a measure of innovation and cost-cutting ideas that, today, would be quite unpalatable.

The political segmentation of Germany meant that the motor industry there was in a far more precarious state than in Britain. Yet the recovery of the German industries was undertaken speedily and effectively. The French motor industry, too, was quick to recover, although without the dramatic rebuilding that was witnessed in Germany. Spain's industry had been disseminated during that country's civil war of 1936–39, and continued to display in the wake of World War II an element of despair. Italy's recovery was also tortuously painful, hindered by raging inflation and a desperate lack of raw materials. In Japan motor building for the private sector was at a virtual standstill; availability of wide sheet steel was at the mercy of American imports, which meant that of the 30,000 or so vehicles built annually until the mid-1950s, the great majority of these were taxicabs and commercial vehicles.

The French *Motocar*

It was from France that a steady stream of unlikely minicars – or *motocars*, as they were known to the French market – emerged directly after World War II. Among the most eccentric was the tiny Mathis, which was unveiled at the Paris Salon in the autumn of 1946. Aerodynamic it certainly was, appearing more like an egg on wheels, two at the front and one trailing. Featuring front-wheel drive, this could have been termed as something of a revolutionary machine, especially with its 707cc water-cooled flat twin engine with individual radiators built into each of the two cylinder heads.

A three-seater, the Mathis could boast only front-wheel braking, which at least was hydraulic; the car's parking brake operated on the single rear wheel. Suspension was courtesy of coil springs and hydraulic dampers, while the body construction comprised just three assemblies that were electrically welded together. Initial claims regarding fuel economy were for 3ltr per 100km, which is approximately 100mpg, although in reality this was more likely to have been 4ltr per 100km, around 70mpg.

In concept the Mathis was adventurous, and the car's styling, created by Jean Andreau, better known for his aerodynamic offerings for Delage and Peugeot, would not have been out of place more than half a century into the future. The design was possibly too unconventional and Mathis, despite several applications to sell the vehicle as well as exhibiting it at various motor shows throughout Europe, was refused permission by the French government to put it into production.

The Paris Salon also introduced the Rovin and Julien minicars, both of which were the cause of much attention in the motoring press. The Rovin, built by brothers Robert and Raoul de Rovin, was a name that French motorists recognized. Builders of cyclecars and motor cycles during the 1920s, the brothers established themselves in the Delaunay-Belleville factory at St Denis, Seine. It was from there that the tiny Rovin D2 emerged, which *The Autocar* rather unkindly referred to as a two-seater roller skate. It is unfortunate that the D2 did look more like a toy car, the prototype that was presented at the Salon having a Cyclops headlamp. Initially, the

D2 was to have had a 260cc air-cooled, single-cylinder engine and a three-speed gearbox driving the rear wheels, but the de Rovin brothers had a change of heart about the power unit and when the car went into production it was fitted with a 425cc water-cooled, flat-twin four-stroke engine. There were some styling changes too, the Cyclops lamp giving way to separate wing-mounted lamps which, arguably, made the car appear even more toy-like.

Sporting all-independent suspension and unitary construction, the D2 managed a top speed of 40mph (64km/h). Its weather protection was rudimentary, but this basic specification did not prevent some 200 vehicles being sold in the first year of production. In 1948 a new model, the D3, was introduced. Using the same 425cc engine and mechanical layout that had graced the D2, the D3 was afforded major restyling over its predecessor. A slab-sided body

design featuring headlamps positioned either side of a false grille replaced the cheeky and curvaceous affair, but it too had only very limited weather protection.

Surprisingly, Rovins remained in production until 1961, by which time the D4 had replaced the D3. The new model, introduced in 1950, had a welcome increase in power, the 10bhp 425cc engine having been enlarged to 462cc, thereby providing 13bhp. The D4's catalogue mentioned speeds in excess of 50mph (80km/h), but in reality the car simply could not be relied upon to provide such performance coupled with any comfort. The D4 had revised frontal styling, in that the headlamps were moved to the top of the wings. That the Rovin survived so long is a mystery, especially as Renault's 4CV and Citroën's 2CV offered relatively luxurious motoring at an affordable price.

Of equally tiny proportions as the Rovin was

The French took the lead in devising some pretty unconventional motocars in the aftermath of World War II. This aerodynamic three-wheeler was designed by Mathis and featured front-wheel drive and a 707cc water-cooled flat-twin engine. (National Motor Museum)

The Rovin depicted here is the D3, which dates from 1948; it was pictured in this rather sorry condition at the 2001 Beaulieu Autojumble.

the Julien, the car's creator being Maurice Julien who had been one of André Citroën's allies in producing the innovative Traction Avant in 1934. The car was powered by a 325cc single-cylinder engine driving the rear wheels via a single chain. A feature of the Julien was that the rear section of the body lifted up to afford easy access to the running gear. Modifications in 1948 produced revised styling very like that of the Rovin, and the engine was increased in size to 360cc. However, production remained small, mainly because it was too much akin to the Rovin, which attracted the majority of sales.

One car that might have become a serious competitor in the *motocar* market was the CHS. This was the product of Chausson, one of France's leading automotive companies, and that country's largest producer of sheet metal stamping. Suppliers of some 80 per cent of all radiators used in the French motor industry, the company was, therefore, well versed in motor body construction. It was proposed that the bodywork be comprised of just two body pressings, each combining one whole side and an equal part of the front and rear assemblies. The interior was destined to be just as simple with seat cushions that were supported on springs and stretched between parts of the main structure, and for the facia panel and electric wiring to be merely clipped into place. Prototype models featured a single-cylinder, water-cooled 350cc engine, front-wheel drive and independent all-round suspension, along with unitary construction. The engine was placed ahead of the radiator, as in Fiat Topolino fashion, steering was of rack and pinion type, and the brakes were cable-operated. Maximum speed of the open two-seater, which weighed just $5\frac{1}{2}$cwt (279kg), was 50mph (80km/h); fuel consumption was said to be around 70mpg (4ltr/100km). However, Chausson was denied the opportunity of putting the CHS into production because the French government considered that the company was better placed to produce buses and coaches, which it did in impressive quantities. There is some evidence that Austin was interested in building the CHS in Britain, but in the event could not negotiate the steel allocation that was necessary to produce the car.

After World War II the French had instigated a national five-year plan to encourage the development of economy cars, and that trend was evident at the Paris Salon held in October 1947. The Boitel was particularly attractive and resembled a full-size car but in miniature, a 500cc water-cooled, two-cylinder two-stroke engine being installed at the rear. Possibly the Rovin, among others, was responsible for the Boitel's dearth of customers, and within three years the model was defunct.

When it was introduced at the 1947 Salon, the diminutive Dolo caused something of a sensation. Having styling characteristics that were eccentric to say the least, the minicar really was more akin to the bubblecar theme that was yet to be seen. Featuring a plexiglass cabin dome and a split windscreen, the Dolo was a two-seater devoid of both luggage space and a child's seat. The shape of the Dolo was undoubtedly adventurous; the bulbous front featured headlamps that were neatly faired into the jaw, while the nose above afforded access to the engine compartment, in which was installed a 571cc air-cooled, flat-four driving the front wheels via a gearbox fitted with an overdrive top ratio. Enclosed rear wheel arches gave a sense of aerodynamics, as did the sharply raked tail.

Delightfully absurd was Charles Mochet's minuscule open two-seater that really did more resemble a child's pedal car. Mochet was prolific in his designs for absolutely minimal transportation, and he carried over to the immediate post-war years his ideas that he had nurtured since 1927. Supported on what appeared like pram wheels, the Mochet 100 was introduced in 1948 with a Zürcher 100cc engine which, in reality, afforded speeds not in excess of 25mph

(40km/h). Suspension of the Mochet was just as simple as the rest of the car, the tyres and frame providing as little springing as could be expected from a bicycle.

The aforementioned Citroën 2CV with its 375cc flat-twin air-cooled engine was, along with the 4CV Renault, prominently displayed within the minicar sections of the early post-war Salons. Both vehicles cannot in any way be classed as minicars, despite the 2CV's tiny motor, nor were they intended as such by their designers.

There was, however, a plethora of minicars that were, at least, announced, and several that made it, just, to the prototype stage of development. These were often the casualties in a rush to provide the most minimal of transportation within the French five-year plan to get the population back on to wheels, whether that be three or four, or occasionally even two. Of the most bizarre types credit must be given to the Reyonnah, which was designed with front wheels that could be folded nearly together so as to be of similar track to those at the rear. Ideal for those awkwardly small parking spaces, and to get the vehicle through doorways, it nevertheless had few other attributes.

The true forerunner of the bubblecar is arguably the L'Oeuf, an egg-shaped battery-powered machine that was designed by Paul Arzens during the war years as a city car in which he could travel around Paris. Arzens was a noted artist, a sculptor and an engineer whose exotic auto designs were recognized by some leading car makers, including Buick and Peugeot. The sculptor designed his 'Electric Egg' as a three-wheeler, the wheels being tiny in proportion to the rest of the car, and with the dome cabin and doors formed from clear plastic and mated to a light alloy rear section. A steering wheel and single pedal were the only controls. When the latter was pressed, the brake was applied; releasing it controlled a resistance that provided the equivalent of three forward speeds. The Electric Egg's performance was impressive given the development of electric vehicles at the time. From a full battery charge it was possible to cover in excess of 60 miles (100km), and the vehicle's maximum speed was around 37mph (60km/h).

Paul Arzens was not alone in believing that electric traction posed certain advantages. In 1942 Louis Renard had unveiled his three-wheeler which had drive to the single rear wheel. This was a most extraordinary looking light-weight machine, having a sloping bonnet and headlamps that were mounted on long beams protruding from the scuttle. With a top speed of 25mph (40km/h) and a range of some 50 miles (80km), Renard announced that he would build 500 cars by the middle of 1941. The exact number of vehicles to have been built is unknown.

Peugeot, too, developed a battery-powered minicar during the war years. Known as the VLV, 377 examples of this lightweight city car were built from 1941 until 1945. The VLV afforded modest performance – a range no greater than between 44 and 50 miles (70–80km) was possible between charges, and the car's top speed was a shade under 19mph (30km/h). Looking something like an upturned bathtub on wheels, the tiny Peugeot *voiturette electrique* afforded austerity transport in the extreme. In fact, with its narrow track rear wheels, lift-up hood and Cyclops headlamp, it set the fashion for a number of mini-cars that emerged during the 1950s.

As unusual as Peugeot's VLV was Gabriel Voisin's Biscooter. Voisin was, of course, one of France's most respected designers, and as a brilliant engineer he was responsible for a series of elaborate and expensive motor cars that carried an affinity with Bentleys and Rolls-Royces. His Biscooter, however, was the most minimal of minicars; built as a monocoque in aluminium, there was an absence of any substantial body-work or weather protection for the two passengers. As to be expected of Voisin, the Biscooter displayed a measure of innovation with front-wheel drive courtesy of a single-cylinder, air-cooled Gnome et Rhône engine of 125cc. Transmission was by chain to universally jointed front half shafts, the gearbox having three forward speeds and reverse. In addition, a reduction gear, when fitted, afforded six forward speeds and two in reverse.

The Biscooter was designed by one of France's most respected car makers, Gabriel Voisin. When displayed at the 1950 Paris Salon the Biscooter was largely ignored and ultimately was built in Spain as the Biscuter. (National Motor Museum)

Gabriel Voisin 1880–1973

Having been appointed a designer working with a Parisian architect in 1897 following studies at the Beaux Arts in Lyon, Gabriel Voisin nevertheless showed more interest in aviation. In 1903 he joined Ernest Archdeacon, the exponent of motoring, steam cars and, later, aeronautics. An encounter with Archdeacon when he was experiencing problems with the carburettor of his Renault cemented an association between the two men, especially as Voisin had been able to trace and correct a fault that no other engineer had been able to identify.

By 1905 Voisin had made his first flight, and a year later established, with the help of Louis Bleriot, his aeronautical business at Boulogne Billancourt, near Paris. The noted sculptor Delagrange commissioned him to build him an aeroplane, which was to become the first aircraft to take off successfully under its own power. Gabriel's brother Charles joined the business in 1907 and together they built aeroplanes for those fortunate enough to enjoy the new sport of flying. When Voisin presented the French Army with the first all-metal aeroplane in 1914, his own success, together with that of aircraft design generally, was assured. After 1918 Voisin dedicated his life to motor cars after his aircraft factory and personnel remained idle following a decline in aircraft building.

Gabriel Voisin was one of the most gifted engineers in automotive history. His cars have often been charged with being idiosyncratic in design but were nevertheless highly successful as sporting machines. Expensive and over-engineered, Voisins were sought by the most discerning of customers, and the cars have regularly been compared with those produced by Bentley and Bugatti.

Gabriel Voisin designed the Biscooter during the late 1940s, but when displayed at the 1950 Paris Salon it received only a lukewarm reception. Being a visionary, Voisin had produced several derivatives of his design, ranging from a single-seater to a four-seater, and even a steam-powered light van. The vehicle had been offered to the French Post Office for postal deliveries, but it appears that postal workers preferred the comfort of Renaults and the almost conventional (by comparison) Citroën 2CV. Ultimately the Biscooter was built in Spain by Autonacional SA of Barcelona, where it was marketed as the Bis-cuter. Fitted with a Villiers 193cc engine in place of the original Gnome et Rhône, some 20,000 examples were produced, making the Biscuter one of the most successful minicars.

Germany Fights Back

The West German motor industry made a surprisingly rapid recovery, which was due mainly to the determined efforts of the population. Eastern Germany's fortunes in this respect were, however, not so marked. The Opel plant was virtually rebuilt and ready for operation by the end of 1945, and Wolfsburg, under direction of the British, was pouring out Volkswagen Beetles to massive demand. The emergence of minicars, however, was slower to materialize.

It was during the late 1940s that German car designers recognized that the popular car of the immediate pre-war era, and those produced following the Armistice, remained beyond the reach of a large proportion of German motorists. Among the first of a series of miniature cars to be announced was the Champion, an open two-seater that had a sports-type body with a rear-mounted single-cylinder two-stroke 250cc German Triumph motorcycle engine. The car's creator was Wilhelm Meyer, the chief engineer of Zahnradfabrik, the gearbox manufacturers, but it was developed by Hermann Holbein, formerly one of BMW's most experienced design engineers and a noted racing driver.

The Champion had no front-wheel braking, the footbrake operating on the rear wheels and mounted inboard on the drive shafts. The parking brake, in similar fashion to a number of cars at the time, and Fiat's Topolino in particular, operated directly on the propeller shaft at the end of the gearbox. The car's maximum speed was 40mph (65km/h) and fuel consumption was around 70mpg (4ltr/100km). Among the car's most favourable qualities was its price, which amounted to about one-third of the price of a German-built Ford Ten. Within a year the car was given a welcome increase of power via a twin-cylinder two-stroke engine of 398cc.

In 1952 Champion introduced the 400, a neat

coupé of stylish but nevertheless tiny proportions that was built by Drauz, the coachbuilding firm more associated after World War II with Porsche, DKW, NSU and Ford. With headlamps faired into the sloping bonnet, and with a cabin having a split windscreen and sharply raked tail, the 400 was available with either a 400cc Ilo engine, or a 450cc Heinkel unit.

Another sports-like minicar was that built by the Kleinschnittgerwerke and which had a single-cylinder engine driving the front wheels. Of striking design, the two-seater nonetheless had toy-like characteristics, especially with its absence of doors. So small was the car that it was possible simply to step into the cabin, the side panels being a continuation of the front wings. A rear-hinged panel at the front of the bonnet lifted upwards to allow access to the engine and running gear, and the headlamps were built into the leading edges of the front wings.

Many of Germany's tiny cars used either Ilo or Zundapp engines, and it was the latter, in the form of a flat-twin, air-cooled, four-stroke 498cc unit, that was installed in the rear of the Trippel SK10 three-seater coupé. An interesting feature about the car was its gull-wing doors, and it has been claimed that this is where the design of the Mercedes 300SL with its gull-wing doors originated. Trippels were seen at various motor shows during 1950 and 1951, but the manufacturer failed to put the car into production in Germany. Instead, it was built in very small numbers in France by Marathon. Both prototype and production SK10s had unorthodox styling ideas, and their semi-enclosed front wings displayed certain aerodynamic features.

Wilhelm Meyer, the maker of Meyra invalid carriages, introduced in 1950 a development of his motorized cars for domestic sales. The Meyra 55 was distinctive in that its styling displayed similarities with the pre-war Goliath Pioneer, and was a tiny three-wheeler with a single wheel at the front. Power was derived from an Ilo 197cc single-cylinder engine driving the rear wheels. Some 300 55s were built before the model was superseded in 1953 by a machine that was of bubblecar appearance.

Of those minicars making an appearance before the end of 1950, Fritz Fend's three-wheeler invalid car and the Fuldamobil were two cars which went on to enjoy long and prosperous careers, and which will be discussed in greater detail in subsequent chapters. The Fend was first introduced in 1948 and was designed as a manually propelled single-seater invalid car. Supported on bicycle wheels, these invalid carriages were hardly car-like, even when fitted with either a 38cc Victoria engine or a 98cc Sachs unit. Smaller wheels were introduced, which made the Fend look more like a minicar, and in addition a larger 100cc Ridel engine became an option. Fritz Fend chose to redesign the concept of his cars in 1953 by introducing a tiny tandem two-seater powered by a 174cc Sachs engine. It was with his Kabinenroller that Fend was to strike up a collaboration that resulted in the cars eventually being developed by Professor Willy Messerschmitt.

The Fuldamobil of 1950 had more to do with caravan construction than cars, perhaps not surprisingly as it was built in a caravan factory. The Fuldamobil was of wooden construction with light alloy panels, with all-steel bodies being introduced in the mid-fifties. Power was delivered by a 250cc Ilo engine, although some early models were fitted with a 360cc Sachs engine; both engines were of single-cylinder configuration and drove the single rear wheel. Fuldamobils underwent considerable development and were marketed in several countries under varying names.

Among the bestselling of Germany's minicars was the Lloyd LP300, a scaled-down car design that was driven via its front wheels by a 10bhp 293cc vertical twin-stroke along with transmission comprising an unsynchronized three-speed gearbox. A variety of body styles was available; these were fitted to a simple backbone chassis which had transverse leaf independent front suspension. The coachwork of the Lloyd was very simple, consisting of a wooden frame with metal corners and covered with leatherette.

The LP300 was fitted with a 386cc engine in 1952, when the car was designated the LP400.

Built of wood and light alloy panels in a caravan factory, the Fuldamobil provided essential motoring for thousands of customers. It featured micro power in the form of either a 250cc Ilo engine or a 360cc Sachs unit. (National Motor Museum)

The Lloyd was highly respected in its native Germany and was among the most popular minicars. Power was courtesy of a 300cc two-stroke engine while the transmission comprised a three-speed crash gearbox. The styling of the car was unlike some other minicars of the period in that it actually looked conventional. (National Motor Museum)

Subsequent Lloyds were fitted with larger engines of 386cc. Note the styling of these LP400 models compared to that of the LP300. (National Motor Museum)

Up until then, in excess of 18,000 vehicles had been sold. Lloyds cost less than the Beetle, but of course did not have the VW's sophistication, and were, for many families, simply too small.

The Italian Job

Before World War II, the Italians had developed a love affair with the minuscule Fiat 500, known affectionately as the 'Topolino', or 'Little Mouse'. The tiny Fiat was, nevertheless, a full-blown motorcar in its own right, merely scaled down in size with a chassis that was designed to help reduce the car's overall weight to a minimum. The Topolino was a two-seater with, so contemporary publicity literature claimed, sufficient space to carry a couple of children sitting on cushions behind the driver's and passenger's seats. All but a few Topolinos were built as convertibles, and there were estate versions too.

The Cinquecento (500A) was introduced in 1936 with a 569cc side valve four-cylinder engine placed ahead of the radiator and driving the rear wheels. When it was superseded by the overhead valve 500B in 1948, in excess of 122,000 vehicles had been built. When the

The most famous of Italian minicars was the Fiat 500. Dante Giacosa, the car's designer, is seen standing alongside the immortal Topolino – 'Little Mouse'. (Fiat)

Dante Giacosa 1905–1996

Dante Giacosa joined SPA (Societa Piemontese Automobili) in 1928, having qualified with a degree in mechanical engineering. When SPA was absorbed into the Fiat empire in 1929, Giacosa was appointed to the company's Lingotto works as a draughtsman. When Fiat sought to introduce the 500, since known affectionately as the Topolino, it was Giacosa who was assigned the task of designing the engine and chassis. The Topolino was planned from the outset as being the most minimal of cars, although Giacosa decided that the chassis and drive train should be largely conventional.

Giacosa understood only too well the philosophy concerning small car design – not only did he ultimately design the Fiat 600 and the tiny Multipla people carrier, he also gave the world the diminutive Fiat 500 Nuova, the Autobianchi Biachina and designs for a micro city-car. The designer was also involved in the concept of a minicar that was inspired by the Piaggio-built Vespa scooter.

When introduced in 1936, the Topolino offered comfortable motoring for two adults. In the absence of a rear seat, children were normally carried sitting on cushions. The Fiat 500 was powered by a 569cc four-cylinder, water-cooled side-valve engine fitted ahead of the gearbox. (Malcolm C. Elder)

500B's engine remained with the restyled 500C that was introduced in 1949, sales of those two models reached nearly 400,000 units by 1955, the year the car was replaced by the equally small Fiat 600, itself a larger version of the considerably smaller Nuova 500 that made its debut in 1957.

The Fiat 500C was an altogether more modern-looking machine than the 500A and 500B. The main difference to its predecessors was some distinctive restyling featuring a full-width frontal treatment with slightly recessed headlamps that were built into the wings. Instead of carrying a spare wheel externally on the tail below the roof or hood, this was now carried in a separate compartment below the boot floor, and the boot itself, which was inaccessible from the outside, was significantly enlarged.

Inside the Topolino all the creature comforts expected to be found on a full-size car were in evidence: hydraulic brakes (the parking brake operated on the transmission rather than the wheels); a heater; comfortable seats; comprehensive instrumentation; and a draught and leak-proof hood that could be collapsed or raised in a trice. There were, however, some economy measures such as sliding windows and an absence of soundproofing, and luggage had to be hauled in and out of the boot via the front-opening doors. The car's minimal dimensions meant that two averagely sized adults would be conveyed on a journey with little or no room to spare width-wise, so shoulder space was, at the best, restricted.

Italy's raging inflation meant that post-war a Topolino cost virtually double its pre-war price. It was, nevertheless, economical on fuel, the 500C averaging 56mpg (5ltr/100km), which was substantially better than the 500A's 47mpg (6ltr/100km). Compared to some minicars, the Topolino was no slouch and could reach 59mph (95km/h), although it made some fuss getting

there. The Fiat's performance was often put to the test under demanding conditions on mountainous roads and under the command of drivers who had the accelerator pedal permanently flat on the floor. The car was a regular rally competitor, often chosen by some of the most noted motor sport enthusiasts of the day, among whom was Earl Howe, then president of the British Racing Drivers' Club.

The tiny car with the huge personality, the Topolino cannot really be claimed as a true minicar, despite it being as small, even smaller, than some of those vehicles under review here. Both functional and comfortable, the Topolino proved to be one of the most successful small cars of all time.

The Fiat Cinquecento, native to Italy, was also built in relatively large numbers in France where it was marketed and sold as the Simca Cinq; when the Fiat 500C was introduced, it emerged as the Simca Six. A version known as the 400 was also built by Fiat (England) Ltd in small numbers at its factory near Wembley. Unlike those cars built in Italy and France, the 400 was designed as a purpose-built four-seater saloon.

In comparison with the Topolino, two of Italy's minicars, the Volugrafo and the Volpe, were minute. The Volugrafo Bimbo, introduced

Post-war 500s were restyled and fitted with ohv four-cylinder engines. The boot space was enlarged so that the spare wheel was carried below the floor.

in 1946, really did look like a dodgem car and measured only 2,400mm (94in) in length, making it one of the tiniest cars in the world. The engine was a 125cc ohv motorcycle affair, and drive was to the left-hand rear wheel via a three-speed gearbox. The Volpe, introduced a year later in 1947, was only 100mm (4in) longer. A two-cylinder, two-stroke 124cc engine afforded a measure of power via an electro-magnetic four-speed gearbox to propel the machine to 47mph (76km/h). Designed as a big car in miniature, the Volpe failed to go into series production owing to a number of difficulties, one being a legal matter. For the Italians, whose love affair with tiny cars had spanned two decades, the Volpe and Volugrafo were, in reality, far too small to be practical.

The 1947 Superveturetta roadster was without doors in prototype form, but in production the model was afforded 'suicide doors' as in the case of the Topolino. The car's rear track was narrower than that at the front, and the 250cc two-stroke twin was mounted above the rear wheels. Had the car's development progressed as intended there would have been a 350cc model, which would be ideal, the makers claimed, for those customers driving in mountainous regions. Another somewhat obscure minicar was the Lucciola, which was a three-wheeler coupé of modern lines. Displayed at the Milan show of 1948, it seems that the car attracted few customers, and the car's makers subsequently went out of business.

Minicars Worldwide

Under the pen of the erudite motoring journalist Gordon Wilkins, *Autocar* magazine in 1948 claimed that minicars were not a family investment aimed at impressing the neighbours, but were more akin to household utensils, as stark as lawn mowers and functional as wheelbarrows. While microcar enthusiasts will possibly show some contempt at such analogies, he arguably had a point. With a need to be cheap to purchase and to operate, minicars also had to be simple to maintain. Of necessity, their manufacture had to

avoid the need for expensive press tools and dies which, at that time, were rarely available. An exhibition held in Prague during the autumn of 1948 revealed a collection of more than two dozen minicars, some of which were so bizarre that development beyond the prototype stage would have been highly unlikely.

Among those cars shown at Prague was the three-wheeled Autocykl, which demonstrated some unique cornering characteristics. At speed it was possible for the coachwork, passengers and front wheel to tilt whilst negotiating fast bends, the power unit and rear axle remaining normally on the road. The vehicle's banking was controlled by the driver operating a pedal linkage. A tiny motor tricycle with a single rear wheel driven via a 350cc air-cooled engine was also displayed; the Czechoslovak Kreibich was basic to say the least, but the bodywork was all-enveloping and featured just one headlamp on the off side of the vehicle.

The Swiss Rapid, built between 1946 and 1951, was the product of Switzerland's leading lawnmower manufacturer. Its performance, courtesy of a tiny air-cooled and rear-mounted MAG single-cylinder opposed 350cc engine that delivered no more than 7bhp, really did not live up to the car's almost sports-like styling. Production ceased after only thirty-six cars had been completed.

The most unlikely market for a minicar in the early post-war years was the USA, where petrol was not rationed and was inexpensive, and where motorists were more accustomed to large cars capable of high cruising speeds. Amidst that climate, however, the Crosley found some fortune, and the marque, which had first appeared in 1939, remained in production until 1942. Built on a 2,032mm (80in) wheelbase, the Crosley was powered by a minute (by American standards) 15bhp air-cooled twin, but in 1946, when production resumed, it was a 717cc engine that was fitted, its origins belonging to a stationary engine design. Having sold in excess of 28,000 vehicles in 1948, Crosley nevertheless abandoned minicar production in 1949 in order to concentrate on full-size cars.

The LONG LOOK

Look at the sweeping lines of the new Crosley Station Wagon, a triumph of designing by Crosley, world's largest producer of station wagons. Practical. Beautiful. Plenty of room for 4 in the roomy body. Remove the rear seat and you have space for a quarter ton load with two huskies riding in front. Upholstered in colorful, long-wearing plastic-coated material. The Crosley Station Wagon is all-steel and comes in a variety of attractive Crosley colors.

The LARGE LOOK

The new Crosley is big! Its startling speed-line styling is so graceful that the whole car is a picture of motion. And the new Crosley Convertible for 4 has all the refinements and deft touches that makes Crosley a FINE car. Big luggage compartment. The easy-to-handle top can be raised or lowered in a jiffy. Upholstered in red plastic material, and lined with water-resistant, plastic material with grain leather look. Yes, the new Crosley Convertible is a car to put a song in your heart, a car that draws admiring glances wherever it goes.

The SMART LOOK

Perfect proportions, a designer's dream, make the Crosley Sedan DeLuxe the smart family car. And when you slip behind the wheel, you discover a truly luxury interior with rich appointments and fine auto upholstery fabric. Roomy—as all Crosley cars are. The Sedan seats four—with plenty of space for luggage. It's available in a striking range of Crosley colors. For going places smartly, drive the new Crosley Sedan DeLuxe.

Microcars were not as popular in America as they were elsewhere, due to adequate supplies of petrol and raw materials, hence the Crosley was the only microcar sold there.

The Larmar was originally designed as an invalid carriage, although some models were built as minicars. Of narrow construction, the Larmar was built to pass through a standard doorway. (Gordon Fitzgerald)

British Minicars Meet Demand

As noted above, in Britain the post-war return to car manufacturing was largely based on pre-war designs. As in Germany, the British were slow to recognize the virtues of the minicar, especially as it was considered to be as expensive to build small cars as it was to assemble larger machines.

Among the first of the post-war minicars to come on to the market was the Larmar, a tiny air-cooled $2\frac{1}{2}$hp single-seater monocar that owed its origins to invalid carriage design. Intended as comfortable and economical transport for one person, the Larmar had a track of just 590mm (1ft $11\frac{1}{4}$in) and a wheelbase of 1,448mm (4ft 9in), which enabled the vehicle (in theory at least) to pass through a standard doorway. Designed and manufactured by Larmar Engineering of Ingatestone, Essex, the car was aimed at providing essential transport for those who were able, as

well as those who were disabled. Having a maximum speed of 35mph (56km/h), it was possible to achieve 65mpg (4.4ltr/100km), and for £198, purchase tax not being applicable, it was among the cheapest vehicles then available.

Not exactly aesthetic in design, the Larmar nonetheless did have some finer features. It could be supplied with conventional controls as well as hand controls, and the turning circle was a tight 15ft. An adaptation of the motorcycle kick-start in the form of a lever operated from within the cabin, and needing only a sharp upward movement, fired the engine into life. Transmission comprised a chain drive to the inside rear wheel, and braking was cable-operated; the minimal electrics, for there was a single headlamp along with twin side and tail lamps, was effected via a chain-driven 6V Lucas dynamo. All in all, the Larmar, despite its shortcomings, did add some character to the motoring scene in what was a pretty gloomy period.

Larmar was not the only manufacturer to sense that there was a possibility for marketing what, essentially, were invalid carriages during times of austerity. The Thames Ditton firm of AC began, in 1947, to build invalid cars for what was then the Ministry of Pensions. These cars should not be confused with the quite different AC Petite that made its appearance in 1953. AC invalid cars were initially fitted with rear-mounted BSA single-cylinder engines, and later were specified with Steyr-Puch engines.

Invacar of Westcliffe-on-Sea, Essex, was another invalid car manufacturer of the same period, producing quite innovative vehicles from 1947 until 1977. BSA 125cc Bantam engines provided the power for the Invacar Mark 1, and later models used a 197cc Villiers engine mated to a four-speed gearbox. Invacar's main rival was the Tippen, built at Coventry between 1950 and 1970. Both Invacar and Tippen carriages became a familiar sight, easily identifiable by their pale blue colour.

The Eaglet, introduced in 1948, might have looked like an invalid carriage, but in fact was an electric three-wheeler that was designed for a top speed of 30mph (48km/h) and to have a range of 30 miles (48km) from a single battery charge. It was expensive at over £400, and only a few were made before the car's demise.

From his factory at Tamworth, Tom Williams resumed building his Reliant three-wheeled vans in 1946, and the first post-war vehicle was delivered on 13 March. A variety of body styles was soon available, including a pick-up and a mobile sales vehicle. Reliant was quick to establish a keen market, and one of the company's first major customers was the LMS Railway with an order for a series of express parcel delivery vans.

Reliant resumed building its three-wheeler van in 1946. Well built and reliable, Reliants were made in a number of body styles, including a mobile shop. (National Motor Museum)

The fact that Reliant had chosen aluminium as a raw material was fortuitous, as it was not rationed in the same way that steel was. Model improvements included a 10cwt (508kg) capacity van that became known as the Regent, and was fitted with Reliant's own engine, which had replaced the pre-war Austin Seven unit.

In 1948 Lawrie Bond, creator of the Bond Minicar, introduced his tiny shopping car when all types of new vehicle were almost unobtainable for the home market. Bond had set himself up in business in 1944 to manufacture vehicle and aircraft components in Blackpool, but had moved to nearby Preston towards the end of the decade, where he spent some of his time designing tiny 500cc racing cars. It was Bond's little shopping car that emerged as one of the most endearing and successful of post-war minicars. Bond and Reliant might have been poles apart in design, but they were nevertheless rivals in the strongly contested market of economy motoring.

3   Battle Royal – Bond Versus Reliant

When the Bond Minicar was introduced in 1948, Reliant was known only for its small three-wheeler commercial vehicles. The unlikely formula of merging motorcycle and motor vehicle technologies had worked to provide what was essentially a unique concept in minimal transport. Likewise, the Bond took on an improbable appearance that was nevertheless greeted with enthusiasm from the motoring press. Looking at those early examples of Reliants and Bonds today, it is almost a miracle that something so utterly utilitarian survived. Survive they did, however, and both marques went on to gather fiercely loyal customers who revered their machines over several decades. What were essentially motorized tricycles became a familiar aspect of the British motoring scene.

When Reliant's first passenger car was introduced in 1953, the year of Queen Elizabeth II's coronation, the Bond had been in production for five years. Why Reliant chose the Regal appellation is obvious, but it also retained a corporate association with the Regent van, and the name was easy to remember and rolled off the tongue. Bond had no aspirations regarding any specific name for its diminutive carriage – a minicar it was, and Minicar it was called.

Bond – Brave New World

Lawrence Bond, better known as 'Lawrie' Bond, was a prolific designer whose tiny 500cc racing cars had achieved notoriety, if little success, by the time he launched his Minicar. Bond's enterprising nature had been responsible for a number of ventures, most of which stemmed from a life

connected with the aviation, steam and motor industries. His experience working with some of the country's leading firms was sufficient for him to establish his own business in 1944 manufacturing components and trading as the Bond Aircraft and Engineering Co. (Blackpool) Ltd.

Bond's expertise in aviation matters was largely responsible for the design of a minicar, which he originally intended as little more than an economical runabout for himself and his wife Pauline. He started work on the design in 1944, and it came to fruition in 1948, when it was introduced as the Mark A. By this time, Bond had moved his business to Longridge, near Preston. One reason for moving from Blackpool was that government contract work, which had been the mainstay of the business, had come to an end, thus allowing Bond to spend some time developing a range of ideas as future projects. Known as Towneley Works, the premises formed part of an old fire station on Berry Lane, and were in fact no more than a small two-storey workshop with a flat above – this became the Bond family home – along with a yard, which was hardly ample in size.

Sketches of Bond's ideas for his Minicar illustrate that aircraft design technology played an important part in keeping the vehicle's weight to a minimum, and when he built the prototype he used sheet aluminium for the stressed-skin bodywork. That the design afforded only the most minimal motoring is very clear, and it has to be appreciated that to become mobile during this time of austerity often meant adopting a measure of innovation.

Although Lawrie Bond had his own workshop, he was without any manufacturing facilities. The

Few early Bonds have survived, which makes this exquisitely restored 1950 Mark A all the more interesting. Power was derived from a Villiers 197cc engine that was built in unit with the gearbox to drive the single front wheel.

Lawrence 'Lawrie' Bond 1907–1974

A Lancastrian, Lawrence Bond grew up in Preston and was the son of the noted artist and historian Frederick Bond. Educated at Preston Grammar School, the young Lawrie served an apprenticeship with Atkinson & Co., the Preston-based heavy vehicle manufacturers. Following a term with Meadows Engineering of Wolverhampton, he went to work in the design department of the Blackburn Aircraft Company at Brough. It was his experience with aeroplane technology and weight-saving techniques that influenced Bond when, later, he turned his attention to motor vehicle design. Having a technical background, Bond was successful in winning government contract orders when he established his own engineering business under the auspices of the Bond Aircraft and Engineering Co. (Blackpool) Ltd.

When government contract orders dried up, Bond had to move from Blackpool to smaller and less expensive premises. It was at Towneley Works at Longridge where he experimented with many ideas, and where he formulated the basics of his tiny three-wheeled runabout that emerged as the Bond Minicar. In addition to small utility vehicles, Lawrie Bond designed racing cars and sports saloons along with water scooters, motor scooters and motorcycles, and even caravans. Additionally, he was the inspiration behind the Opperman Unicar and the Berkeley sportscar.

Reliant took over Bond Cars in 1969 and ultimately closed the latter's factories. The Bond name did live on for a time, however, when Reliant introduced its fun car, the Bond Bug.

Towneley Road premises were so inadequate that Bond had constructed his Minicar on the upper floor of the workshop and lowered it through a trap door on to the ground floor. When he met Colonel Gray, managing director of Sharp's Commercials, also based in Preston, Bond sensed the opportunity of putting his Minicar into production. (During the mid-1950s the apostrophe was dropped from the name so that it became Sharps, the spelling hereafter used.) Similarly to the Bond Aircraft and Manufacturing Co., Sharps Commercials was also at the mercy of diminishing orders under the government contract scheme, but the firm was well versed in the automotive business. As assemblers of Chevrolet vehicles destined for the British Army under an agreement with the USA, Sharps was also a designated repairer and renovator of military vehicles under the Auxiliary Army Workshop scheme.

Having seen and tried the prototype Minicar, and no doubt having been spurred on by some favourable press reports, Colonel Gray warmed to the idea of putting the vehicle into production. However, he did have some concerns regarding aspects of the car's styling and technical specification, and it was only after Bond had agreed to some modifications that the arrangement materialized.

When interviewed about his involvement with Lawrie Bond and his Minicar, Colonel Gray remembered that Bond had asked him whether he would agree to lease the Sharps factory to him in order that he could put his vehicle into production. Gray had some eighty or ninety people working for him at the time, and decided not to rent the factory but would instead undertake to build the Minicar on Bond's behalf. Colonel Gray, appreciating that motorcycle combinations did not always present the most suitable means of travel, anticipated there to be a demand for Bond's design, and therefore took a gamble on it being attractive to motorcycle-weary families.

The Bond Minicar had first been mentioned in the motoring press late in May 1948, and this was due in part to Pauline Bond's media skills – having worked in Fleet Street, she knew the most direct routes to an editorial desk. *The Motor* featured the car as the 'New runabout at under £200' and showed it being driven by Lawrie with Pauline as passenger. The car was again appraised in the following November when *Autocar* ran a feature on it alongside Bond's Type C 500 racing car and disclosed that it was already in production with a planned output of fifty vehicles a week (in reality, production got under way with no more than fifteen cars a week).

Although in retrospect the Bond prototype now appears quite stylish, with its almost art-deco appearance, its construction was distinctly utilitarian. Having no chassis, the styling incorporated a large louvre air-intake at the front, and the two 6V headlamps that were attached high up on the body sides adjacent to the rear-hinged bonnet opening appeared as something of an afterthought. The engine that Bond had proposed was a 122cc Villiers unit with integral three-speed gearbox. This was mounted directly on the steering fork, and drive was effected to the single front wheel via a secondary chain so that wheel and engine assembly turned as a single unit. The cable and bobbin steering was of the same design as that used on Bond's 500cc racing cars, and the cable-operated brakes worked on the tiny rear wheels only. Bond had anticipated that such modest performance derived from the Villiers motorcycle engine would not call for particularly sophisticated braking; nor was there any rear suspension other than that afforded by the low-pressure tyres.

The prototype's cruising speed was shown to be around 30mph (50km/h) although it was indicated that 40mph (65km/h) was possible under favourable conditions. Climbing hills did not pose any problems for the little car, which proved that it could cope with 1 in 4 gradients with ease. The weight of the car was a mere 200lb (90kg), which meant that it could be lifted off the ground quite effortlessly by just two people. Lawrie Bond's attention to detail in racing car design meant that the Minicar's controls were light and precise in use, the gear selector lever requiring only the lightest finger touch in operation. Contrary to popular belief, the

The Morecambe Rally was a regular event that attracted a wide diversity of vehicles. This Mark A Bond gets under way along the sea front to the amusement of rally officials. The Minicar's diminutive size is apparent in this evocative photograph taken in 1952. (National Motor Museum)

Bond did not have a kick-starter; starting was effected via a hand control in the cabin. Economy being all essential, fuel consumption was claimed to be in excess of 100mpg (3ltr/100km), a definite advantage during petrol rationing.

It was early 1949 before the Minicar went into production at Sharps Commercials' factory off Ribbleton Lane in Preston. By this time, Colonel Gray had negotiated a deal with Lawrie Bond and had agreed to pay the designer a nominal amount for each car that was produced. Ultimately, Bond decided to sell the manufacturing rights of his Minicar to Sharps Commercials who undertook to retain the Bond name, and Bond himself was retained on a consultancy basis regarding design matters.

The Minicar that emerged from Ribbleton Lane displayed a number of differences to Lawrie Bond's prototype. The nose of the car had been significantly restyled to incorporate more rounded features, and there was evidence of a

Bond Minicar (De-Luxe)	
Chassis	
Type	Integral
Engine	
Layout	Air-cooled, single-cylinder
Peak power	8.4bhp @ 4,000rpm
Bore×stroke	59×72mm
Cubic capacity	197cc
Compression ratio	8:1
Fuel supply	
Carburettor	Villiers 2-lever; gravity feed fuel; oil with fuel lubrication
Electrical	
Battery	6V, 10amp/hr
Transmission	
Clutch	Single plate
Gearbox	Three-speed integral with engine
Drive	Enclosed chain primary drive; final drive via chain to front wheel
Steering	
Type	Cable and bobbin, replaced by rack and pinion
Brakes	
Front	None
Rear	5in drum brakes, mechanically operated
Suspension	
Front	Coil spring
Rear	None
Shock absorber	Andre friction
Tyres	
Type	Goodyear 16×4in
Capacity	
Fuel tank	11.4ltr (2½gal)
Weight	
Unladen kerb weight	3¼cwt (165kg)
Performance	
Top speed	43.3mph (70km/h)
Fuel consumption	72mpg (4ltr/100km)

discreet bumper that, while affording some protection, also accommodated the registration plate. The headlamps were set further back towards the scuttle, but the perspex windscreen, which was a constant source of complaint, remained. On the prototype, the rear wheels had been semi-enclosed, whereas the production car sported flared wheel arches. The cockpit was slightly less austere, but still provided little in the way of big-car creature comforts.

Similarly to Bond's prototype, the production model, which later was designated the Type A Minicar, did not feature doors owing to the vehicle's method of lightweight monocoque construction. However, despite the car's diminutive size, its absence of doors did little to facilitate easy entry and exit. Nor was there sufficient accommodation for any significant luggage behind the seats, although it was claimed otherwise.

It became apparent to those in charge of production that the Minicar's cable and bobbin steering was not particularly reliable and that some modification was necessary. Potentially, the car attracted those customers who carried out their own maintenance, especially ex-motorcyclists, but even for them the steering arrangement was a fiddly business to keep in good order. When rack and pinion steering was introduced as an option on production cars, there were a number of owners who were keen to carry out the conversion themselves, or have it professionally fitted at their own garage.

Improved Bonds

When *The Motor* put the Bond through a gruelling trial in the spring of 1950 it was the Minicar De-Luxe that was tested. The model had been introduced earlier in the year with an enlarged engine, and features such as a hydraulic front shock absorber and an electrically operated windscreen wiper, both of which were welcomed by customers who put comfort and efficiency before total economy. Evident too, was rack and pinion steering which was now standardized throughout Bond production.

Another feature was the more substantial triplex curved windscreen which at last addressed those complaints from owners who found that the previous type of perspex screen became opaque with use. It also formed the anchorage for the side screens and hood, which, once raised, afforded full weather protection.

The Motor reported a significant increase in performance with the larger 197cc Villiers engine. Acceleration from 0–30mph was achieved in 13.6 seconds, a figure that was *only* (this was *The Motor*'s emphasis) 40 per cent greater than an 8HP post-war saloon. A stable ride was afforded along with steering that was as light as a feather, and corners could be taken at speed without there being any swaying motion. Even when a kerb was clipped at speed and the offending wheel was bounced into the air, the car stayed on course without problem.

The single-cylinder air-cooled, two-stroke engine came in for some praise from *The Motor*'s test drivers who found the hand-lever-operated 'kick-start' particularly easy to use, especially when employed in conjunction with the compression release pedal. Such engines naturally were without the smoothness of a four-cylinder four-stroke, but nonetheless the Villiers unit performed admirably both under pressure in London traffic and in the more relaxed surroundings of the countryside.

More Improvements – The Mark B Bond

On 1 July 1951 Sharps Commercials announced the introduction of the Mark B Bond Minicar. Nearly 2,000 Mark A cars had been sold and there appeared to be no shortage of customers. In fact, as soon as the car had been introduced two years previously at the London Cycle and Motorcycle Show it had created so much attention that Sharps were inundated with orders, and Colonel Gray had to recruit additional staff to cater for demand. The Mark B incorporated all the modifications that were made to the previous model, and significant additional features included the introduction of rear suspension, the adoption of increased luggage space and improved weather protection.

Sharps could now confidently claim that its

Bond Minicar featured all-round independent suspension, had better visibility courtesy of its triplex curved screen, and was even easier to start thanks to the adoption of an automatic decompressor. The redesigned bodywork not only provided greater luggage capacity but, as advertisements declared, there was sufficient space for a child's seat. Sharps had also paid attention to the hood, redesigning it to allow greater headroom, and at the same time improving the structure of the windscreen assembly, which, being more rigid than previously, was fitted with a Sorbo rubber pad on to which the hood snugly clamped.

The Villiers 197cc engine was retained, which gave the Minicar a top speed of around 50mph (80km/h) – that is if anyone was sufficiently brave to attempt such a pace. The car's published cruising speed was 40mph (65km/h) along with a miserly fuel consumption of between 85 and 90mpg (3.3–3.1ltr/100km), a figure that was contested by at least one motoring journal. At the time of the Mark B's introduction, petrol rationing had been abandoned, but this nevertheless did not prevent motorists from wanting the most economical transport.

That the Bond Minicar was capable of undertaking continental touring on a grand scale was successfully demonstrated by motoring journalist C.J. Tipper when he embarked on a 9,200-mile (14,800km) expedition that encompassed distances as far south as Madrid, and northwards to Stockholm. Tipper admitted that friends had shown some scepticism that his fragile-looking car would make the journey, especially when negotiating some of Europe's worst roads. But complete his mission he did, with outstanding reliability on behalf of the Bond.

The Mark C Bond

Some 3,000 Mark Bs were built before the completely restyled Mark C made its debut in September 1952 at the Cycle and Motor Cycle Show at London's Earls Court. A prototype had been shown a year previously and at the time had attracted much attention. The car was put into limited production during the following month and for a short period both Mark Bs and Mark Cs emerged from Sharps' assembly line. The last of the Mark Bs left Ribbleton Lane in December, thus fulfilling outstanding orders.

The Mark C was given front wings that extended the length of the bonnet as far as the scuttle. The redesigning process afforded a measure of streamlining so that the bonnet drooped neatly at the front to incorporate a car-like air-intake grille. The headlamps were no longer perched halfway along the bonnet sides and now were sensibly incorporated into the wings. The car could at last be claimed as being a proper 2+2, although the rear seating was definitely cramped and could only accommodate small children.

The passenger cabin remained faithful to Lawrie Bond's original design, although it was now all the more practical by having a door, on the passenger side. If the false wings gave the car more of a grown-up look, it wasn't entirely for aesthetics. Modifications to the steering assembly had meant adoption of the worm and sector arrangement and the facility for the wheel to turn through 180 degrees lock to lock. The increased width at the front of the car that the false wings afforded allowed for the modified steering mechanism to perform its almost eccentric pirouettes.

A particular aspect of the car that had been the cause of some customer dissatisfaction was the absence of reverse gear. This had been omitted in the interests of those owners who held motor-cycle licences, which did not permit driving a three-wheeler with reverse gear fitted. Sharps

The Bond's light weight is being demonstrated to good effect. According to Bond publicity it was possible to change a rear wheel simply by supporting the car against one's thigh. (National Motor Museum)

The Bond Mark C was introduced in 1952 at the London Cycle and Motor Cycle Show. Revised styling is obvious in the car's frontal aspect along with the separate front dummy wings. The latter was devised to allow modifications to the steering mechanism that would enable the car to be turned through 180 degrees.

Bond Mark C

Engine

Layout	Single-cylinder, two-stroke Villiers Mark 6E
Bore×stroke	59×72mm
Cubic capacity	197cc
Ignition	Villiers flywheel magneto

Electrical

Battery	6V, 10amp/hr

Steering

Type	Exposed worm and sector

Suspension

Front	Coil spring and telescopic damper
Rear	Stub axles with trailing arms together with bonded rubber suspension

Brakes

Front	Cable, mechanically operated
Rear	Rods, mechanically operated

Tyres

Type	4.00×8in

Capacity

Fuel tank	11.3ltr (2½gal)

Dimensions

Length	2,997mm (9ft 10in)
Width	1,448mm (4ft 9in)
Wheelbase	1,676mm (5ft 6in)
Track	1,346mm (4ft 5in)
Weight	209kg (460lb)

Performance

Top speed	50mph (80km/h)
Fuel consumption	85–90mpg (3.32–3.13ltr/100km)

Improved weather protection was a welcome bonus to Bond owners. Note that the Mark C was fitted with a door on the passenger side.

The spartan interior of the Mark C Minicar.

had therefore devised a bizarre arrangement consisting of a reversing handle that could be attached to a square boss on the off-side rear wheel and manually operated via a ratchet mechanism to manoeuvre the car rearwards. Needless to say, because of the car's light weight most drivers found it more simple merely to manhandle the car rearwards. The modified steering mechanism did away with the need for reverse as the car could turn within its length, and even be driven backwards without having to rely on a reverse gear. The facility to steer into the tightest parking spaces was soon appreciated by owners, and on many occasions provided onlookers with some amusement.

Other significant changes concerned the bodyshell which featured a redesigned bulkhead and more effective strengthening. Whilst this provided increased protection for passengers in the event of an accident, it also supported the recently modified front suspension. The car's rear suspension – or rather the lack of it – had also been the cause of some criticism from owners, and this was addressed with the introduction of the Mark C. Trailing arms and rubber 'flexitor' units (which were exclusive to Bond and were attached via steel housings to the underside of the car) provided the solution, while also doing away with the need for maintenance or lubrication. Instead of being formed in metal, the rear wings were made of glass fibre and incorporated the now obligatory twin rear lights.

The light weight of the car prompted Sharps not to include a lift jack as part of the car's equipment. The method of changing a wheel was, according to the manufacturer, simple enough – merely slacken the wheel nuts and lift the offending corner of the car on to a suitable stand. As *The Autocar*'s road tester discovered, it was far easier, once the wheel nuts had been slackened, to lift the car and support the offending corner on one's thigh in order to change a wheel. There appeared in *The Autocar* the now famous image of a female member of the journal's test team attempting this task. No one, it appears, ever mentioned what to do in the event of the front wheel being punctured!

The Mark C was the first of the Bond Mini-cars to employ front-wheel braking, an essential modification that for too long had been missing. The same Villiers 197cc 6E engine was utilized, and at long last was fitted with a self-starter that

1954 Monte Carlo Rally contestants Lieutenant M. Crosby and Captain T. Mills with their cream-coloured Bond Mark C. The 197cc-engined car performed superbly throughout the event, with an overall fuel consumption of 63mpg (5ltr/100km). The only non-standard fittings were navigation lights, fog lamps and windscreen demister. (National Motor Museum)

Well-Travelled Bonds

Testament to the Bond's capabilities was the unofficial entry of a Mark C in the 1954 Monte Carlo rally by two army officers, Lieutenant Colonel M. Crosby and Captain T. Mills. It took the pair three and a half days to travel the 2,000 miles (3,200km) from Glasgow to Monte Carlo without any untoward incident before embarking on the home journey.

Douglas Ferreira was another exponent of the Bond Minicar. Having bought a Mark B in1952 in which he travelled thousands of miles including a run from John o' Groats to Lands End, he bought a brand new Mark C on leaving the Merchant Navy and immediately embarked on a European holiday. Douglas drove the car to Rome and Naples in the depth of winter before travelling to the Winter Olympics at Cortina, taking as his route some mountain passes that had been officially closed. Continuing to Austria and Vienna, the car performed admirably, even in temperatures as low as −25°C.

When Bond director Colonel Gray heard of his exploits, Douglas was invited to join the company as its sole sales representative. In this role he visited every one of Bond's 365 dealers throughout Britain and Ireland, using Bond Minicars as his means of transport. During his time working for Bond, Douglas reckons he covered in excess of 350,000 miles (563,000km); recalling those days, he was appointed on a salary of £500 per annum and commission of 5 shillings (25p) for every car that he sold. Today, Douglas is well known within Bond circles and undertakes to judge enthusiasts' cars at the Bond Owner's annual meeting at Morecambe. Naturally Douglas attends in his Mark D.

Douglas Ferreira's Mark C pictured in Rome in the mid-1950s. (Douglas Ferreira)

was offered on the deluxe model but not on the standard car. Changes to the braking and steering arrangements meant that it was necessary to devise a new steering fork. This was made from tubular steel and bolted to the newly modified bulkhead. In order to protect the Minicar's cabin from engine vibration, the engine was treated to an insulated torque stay. Problems encountered with correct drive-chain tension were also addressed, and a trailing arm was employed which pivoted in line with the drive sprocket.

Modifications and Additions

Throughout the life of the Mark C there were some useful modifications and additions to the model range. A Minitruck with an extended body was built to attract commercial users, and the same basic body arrangement formed the basis of the Family Safety Model which, it was claimed, could accommodate five people. In the event the two rear seats were sideways facing, comprising a simple hammock design, which in fact was only suitable for young children. The front bench seat could seat three persons, or so it was claimed, which gave rise to Bond's rather adventurous advertising. A number of minor improvements appeared from time to time, such as uprated electrics, and many of these revisions were made available to owners of existing models.

At the time of the Mark C's introduction at the 1952 London Cycle and Motor Cycle Show, two other three-wheelers were making their debut. One was the AC, more of which later; the other was the Tamworth-built Reliant Regal.

The Regal Makes its Debut

When the Regal was officially introduced at the 1952 London Cycle and Motor Cycle Show, some 3,000 Reliant commercial vehicles had been produced at the company's Two Gates factory. The Regal was purposely designed as a four-seater minicar and its construction differed to that of the Regent van. A box-section chassis was specified, and other car-like features included a conventional steering box, torsion bar suspension for the front wheel which was suspended on a rear-hinged arm, and steering movement, via a conventional wheel, which employed a kingpin. Reliant's own 747cc engine was used, together with the four-speed gearbox that was to be found on the Regent van.

The radiator, engine and running gear were positioned aft of the single front wheel and well back in the chassis so as to afford ideal weight distribution. The spare wheel was positioned above the front wheel, and as such, together with a bulkhead separating the front compartment from the engine bay, offered some front-end protection to passengers in the event of an accident.

Reliant's experience in building aluminium bodies on a hardwood frame came to the forefront with the Regal, which was initially marketed as a convertible only. Unlike the early Bonds, it possessed such luxury items as doors and was a true four-seater, even if there was precious little room for rear occupants. Period advertisements show the Regal with a full complement of passengers, those sitting over the car's rear axle appearing perched somewhat precariously on the narrow bench. Compared to some utility vehicles the Regal offered a measure of sophistication and a degree of comfort. Front bucket seats had fore and aft adjustment, and pivoted forwards to allow access to the rear seat. A toughened glass windscreen, an electrically operated wiper and electric starter were standard equipment. Instrumentation was comprehensive – along with a speedometer there was a fuel gauge and oil pressure indicator, all three being housed in a simple console with a panel light on the facia to the right of the driver.

The Regal went on sale for £299 10s, increasing to £467 7s 10d with purchase tax. Weighing under 8cwt (406kg) and being a three-wheeler, the car, like the Bond, attracted £5 per annum road tax, the sum normally applicable for motorcycles. That, and the money saved on running costs by having to replace only three tyres instead of four was, for a number of years, one of Reliant's marketing ploys.

Reliant Regal Mark 1

Chassis

Type	Box section, pressed steel with tubular braced cross members

Engine

Layout	Four cylinders; side valves
Head material	Cast iron mounted on aluminium crankcase
Peak power	16bhp @ 4,000rpm
Bore×stroke	56×77mm
Cubic capacity	745.5cc

Electrical

Battery	6V

Steering

Type	Burman-Douglas

Suspension

Front	Torsion bar to front wheel
Rear	Long semi-elliptic rear springs on 'Silentbloc' type bushes
Shock absorber	Double acting all round

Brakes

Front	Hydraulically operated drums
Rear	Handbrake acting on rear wheels

Tyres

Size	4.50×14in

Dimensions

Length	3,124mm (10ft 3in)
Width	1,372mm (4ft 6in)
Wheelbase	1,880mm (6ft 2in)
Track	1,143mm (3ft 9in)
Weight	404kg (890lb)

Performance

Top speed	60mph (97km/h)
Fuel consumption	50mpg (5.7ltr/100km)

When *Motor Cycling* tested the Regal there was praise for the car's sturdy construction, its positive Burman-Douglas steering layout and for the performance of the hydraulic braking system. Subsequent reports questioned the intrusion of the engine and the non-synchromesh gearbox

into the passenger compartment, which, apart from the space that was taken up, was the source of some noise. Reliant's engineers, having been concerned about this very issue, took as much precaution as possible to reduce the level of noise within the cabin.

The Regal's performance was more akin to the average small saloon of the time, and therefore was all more impressive when compared with the Bond with its tiny air-cooled engine. According to some reports the vehicle's uncompromising rear suspension made for some discomfort, especially on longer journeys; on anything other than the smoothest of road surfaces the jolting was considerable. On the other hand, the front suspension's well-controlled action met with complete acceptability.

Late in 1954 Reliant introduced the Regal Mark II for the 1955 model year. Some minor styling changes were made, but the car's rather angular shape remained essentially the same as its predecessor, which became known as the Mark I. Most obvious was the softer styling treatment afforded to the car's frontal aspect. The 'cheese grater' grille was replaced by a flush and reshaped air-intake, and to avoid the need for hand signals semaphore trafficators were fitted to the front wings immediately below the scuttle. While the Regal was specified as a drophead coupé, Reliant introduced an optional glass-fibre hardtop model that afforded much in the way of increased comfort. In 1956 with introduction of the Regal Mark III, aluminium coachwork was abandoned altogether in favour of glass fibre. The Regent van was discontinued in favour of a Regal-based commercial vehicle, signalling the demise of Reliant's motorcycle influence.

With its substantial restyling the Regal Mark III was quite a revelation. Gone was the angular shape of the earlier models, replaced by an aesthetically sculptured vehicle featuring full-width styling that incorporated the suggestion of separate front wings along with a deftly shaped air-intake. The new cuddly shape of the Mark III along with its revised interior styling and new facia obviously attracted customers, and during the two years that the model was in production

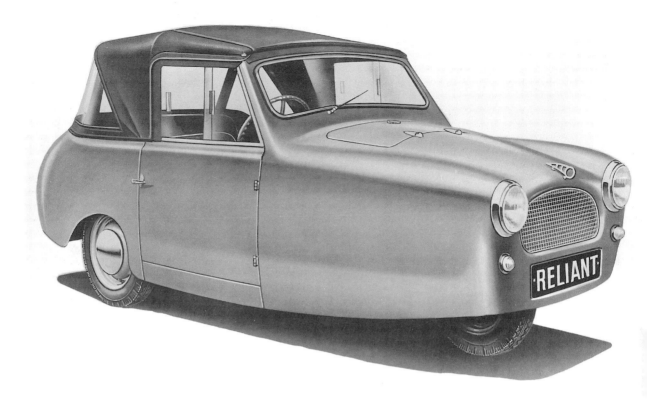

Reliant introduced the Regal three-wheeler in 1952. On the Mark III, introduced in 1956, glass fibre replaced aluminium. The shape of the car was also all the more aesthetic compared to the earlier angular models. Reliant's own 747cc engine was fitted, giving 16bhp maximum power at 4,000rpm. In production for two years, nearly 3,000 Mark III's were sold. (National Motor Museum)

2,798 vehicles were sold. Add this figure to the 1,298 Mark IVs that were sold – the only differences between the two models were winding windows and separate flashing indicators – and they outsold all previous production by some 135 per cent.

The car was constructed so that the moulded glass-fibre body was supported by a timber frame. The roof and rear section could be simply detached by the removal of nine screws and five bolts. The wide, front-hinged doors were fitted with detachable steel-framed windows, each having perspex panels, the middle section sliding to open and close.

The Mark IV had been in production for a year when the Mark V was introduced in 1959. Some of the Mark IV's curvaceous styling gave way to a slightly more angular shape, but this did not prevent the model selling in relatively large numbers – 4,772 Mark Vs were built, thus outselling the combined production of Mark IIIs and IVs by 676. Succinct styling touches meant that the car looked larger than it actually was, and

modifications to the interior with its central instrument console helped to streamline the build process, especially when it came to assembling left-hand-drive models. Most significant about the Mark V was that for the first time Reliant three-wheelers featured external boot access. Oddly, however, winding windows were abandoned in favour of the previous sliding type.

When Reliant introduced some minor styling changes to the Mark V they were deemed sufficiently important to attract the Mark VI designation. Sliding windows remained a feature, and peculiarly the company reverted to combined sidelights and turn indicators. Look at the car in profile and evident is a modified roofline with a pronounced lip over the rear window. When *Motor Cycling* appraised the Mark VI, the tester overdid the rhetoric when it was suggested the car could be driven in sports car style!

Reliant was clearly aiming at two markets – those families fortunate enough to afford a second car, and motorcyclists whose family needs had outgrown a combination sidecar. The company's publicity material was often evocative in style and showed happy family scenes in addition to suggesting the Regal three-wheeler's appeal to lady drivers.

Despite the introduction of the Mini in 1959 the Regal Mark VI, in production between 1961 and 1962, found 8,478 customers, which is almost equivalent to the combined output of the Marks III, IV and V.

Better Bonds

In the same year that the Reliant Mark III made its debut, Bond introduced the Mark D Minicar. At first glance the new model appeared much the same as its predecessor, but was characterized by a modified air-intake grille. A further styling deviation was the enlargement of the glass-fibre rear wings on the family model. Under the bonnet, modifications extended to the engine, with the Villiers 9E replacing the 6E, and an improved clutch facilitated easier gear changing.

Within a year of its introduction Bond replaced the Mark D's three-speed gearbox with a four-speed unit, which, with superior transmission, provided enhanced reliability. 12-volt electrics enabled push-button starting, and the Dynastart system even allowed the engine to be engaged in reverse direction (via a switch on the facia), thereby allowing an effective reverse gear. Bond nevertheless took the precaution of optionally allowing the engine to be started in forward mode only, which avoided any confusion on the part of some owners. Tougher rear suspension courtesy of modified trailing arms and Flexitor units afforded greater durability.

The Dynastart was in effect a combined generator and starter built as a single unit. It transformed the Bond, for at last it afforded easy starting as well as an efficient electrical system that gave improved power to the rather feeble headlamps. Battery charging, too, was improved, thus depriving owners of one more item with which to concern themselves.

The Mark V Regal made its debut in 1959 with restyled bodywork. Minor changes heralded the introduction of the Mark VI, the main identifying feature being the pronounced lip over the rear window. Reliant reverted to sliding windows for both the Mark VI and Mark VI. (National Motor Museum)

Bond announced a new Minicar in 1956 to replace the Mark C. The Mark D featured a new grille, and beneath the bonnet the Villiers 9E engine superseded the 6E. Bond engineers devised a clutch modification to improve gear changing. The Mark C and its successor are seen together; in the background is an Isetta bubblecar.

The Mark D Bond Minicar having been in production for a year, the three-speed gearbox was supplanted by a four-speed unit. Engines were fitted with the 12V Dynastart device to improve starting and to afford reverse motion.

Douglas Ferreira's Mark D Bond being transported for repairs to its engine mounting. Douglas lives close to the Ravenglass and Eskdale Railway in the Lake District, and it proved easier to convey the car to Ravenglass by train. A 15in gauge miniature railway, the R&ER extends several miles inland from the Irish Sea coast at Ravenglass to Boot in the Cumbrian Fells. (Douglas Ferreira)

Bond, similarly to Reliant, had discovered the sales advantage of making available a glass-fibre replacement for the standard hood, and offered customers more substantial weather protection for a mere £25.

When petrol rationing was introduced in December 1956 in response to the Suez crisis, the demand for Bond Minicars escalated. Sharps had intended launching its all-new Minicar, the Mark E, but deferred doing so in order to maintain full production of the Mark D. Prototype models of the Mark E had been unveiled at the London Motor Cycle Show at the end of 1956, but it was early 1958 before production

commenced. What customers saw was an entirely restyled Minicar with full-width frontal styling, a high straight-through wing line, larger headlamps, slab sides, proper doors and an enlarged boot, albeit with no external access. It was longer, too, than the old model, by 300mm (12in), and the frame was a steel rectangular affair, thus making the construction part-integral.

Between announcing the Mark E and putting it into full-scale production, Sharps had experienced some serious problems with the car's handling. In rectifying a tendency for the car to overturn while cornering, Sharps' engineers shortened the wheelbase and widened the rear track, but there remained some concern over the vehicle's performance. Of greater weight than the Mark D, the Mark E with the Villiers 9E engine suffered sluggish acceleration and a reduced top speed. Criticism regarding the car's lethargic performance induced Sharps to introduce the Mark F within eleven months.

During this unhappy period Sharps maintained production of the Mark D until the early months of 1959, by which time the new and larger engined Mark F was fully established. Specified with a glass-fibre top – a convertible

model remained available for those customers requiring it – the Mark F was even heavier than its underpowered predecessor, and in compensation was equipped with the Villiers 246cc Mark 31A two-stroke engine. Mated to a four-speed gearbox, this gave the car a 55mph (89km/h) top speed and an average fuel consumption of between 50–60mpg (5.7–4.7ltr/100km).

When *Motor Cycling* tested the Mark F, its test driver succeeded in pushing the Minicar to its limits and noted that 'A little discretion was required to avoid the inside back wheel lifting on acute bends taken at inordinately high speed.'

Mark C and Mark D Family models had increased accommodation by providing two side-facing seats behind the front bench seat. Narrow and hardly comfortable, the rear compartment seats were designed for children. Family models had extended rear wings that were formed in glass fibre. (National Motor Museum)

The completely restyled Mark E Minicar was unveiled late in 1956 but did not enter production until early 1958. Larger than the earlier models, the Mark E had doors on both sides of the vehicle. Development of the car produced some difficulties for Bond engineers due to some negative handling characteristics that took some time to rectify. (National Motor Museum)

The Mark E Bond was designed to look more like a conventional car. (National Motor Museum)

Bond Mark F	
Chassis	
Type	Light steel box and channel sections
Engine	
Layout	Villiers Mark 31A/4 two stroke
Peak power	12bhp @ 4,500rpm
Bore × stroke	66 × 72mm
Cubic capacity	246cc
Compression ratio	7.5:1
Electrical	
Generator and starter	12V Dynastart combined dynamo and starter
Suspension	
Front	Flexitor bonded rubber; single trailing arm with Armstrong hydraulically controlled coil spring element
Dimensions	
Length	3,353mm (11ft)
Width	1,524mm (5ft)
Wheelbase	2,006mm (6ft 5in)
Performance	
Top speed	51mph (82km/h)
Fuel consumption	81–92mpg (3.49–3.207ltr/ 100km)

There was, however, little need for alarm, for the tester's reassuring comment was that 'In any event, the front bumper would act as a skid long before the overturning position was reached.'

Sharps introduced two Mark F variants in 1960, the Ranger van with a lift-up rear window, and an estate car conversion, the latter being nothing more sophisticated than the Ranger with windows and a full height opening tailgate. Such conversions proved popular and were eventually adopted as standard body styles, although the traditional tourer remained available.

Bigger Bonds – Competing with Reliant

The rivalry between Bond and Reliant came to the fore with the introduction of the Bond 250G in September 1961. Employing the Mark F's power train, the Bond was now marketed as a full four-seater, which was made possible by increasing the size of the passenger compartment without changing the car's overall dimensions. This was achieved by moving the windscreen and front seats forward to allow a full-width rear seat to be fitted in place of the two opposed occasional seats. The roof line was also altered by fitting a reverse angle rear window, as introduced

Within a year of the Mark E's introduction, Bond announced the Mark F largely to answer criticism in respect of the former's sluggish performance. The Mark F pictured here was used by Bond for publicity purposes and for a time served as Douglas Ferreira's company transport. The two young ladies alongside the car worked in the Bond office at Preston. The photograph was taken at Tarn Hows in the Lake District. (Douglas Ferreira)

The Bond Mark F was fitted with the Villiers 246cc two-stroke engine. Performance was improved over the Mark E and provided a top speed of 55mph (89km/h).

Interior of the Bond Mark F. Controls and instruments were sparse.

The Villiers Mk 31A two-stroke engine was fitted to the Mark F. Note the integral gearbox.

on the Ford Anglia and Classic models and on Citroën's 2CV derivative, the Ami 6, in order to provide increased rear headroom and enhanced rear vision. The popularity of the Estate and Ranger body styles meant that these became available from 1962 under the guise of the Bond 250G. Further modifications included provision of wind-up windows, front quarterlights, revised interior trim and larger wheels. On the mechanical side the rear suspension was modified in favour of trailing arms, coil springs and hydraulic shock absorbers; hydraulic braking was also introduced with 7in drums all round.

The same 'cut-back' rear window was employed by Reliant when introducing the all-new Regal 3/25 saloon late in 1962 for the 1963 model year. Dramatically restyled, the Regal 3/25 afforded larger car comfort, accommodation and luggage capacity (with an external opening boot) in minicar guise and economy. While the Bond

scored on economy over the Reliant, the latter was nevertheless much more athletic and could achieve 63mph (100km/h) compared with the Bond's 50–52mph (80–84km/h).

Addressing the competition, Sharps introduced in 1963 the Bond 250G Twin Minicar, which, in place of the usual single-cylinder two-stroke engine, featured Villiers' 4T 249cc twin-cylinder unit. Aware that not all customers wanted such dizzy power that the 14.6bhp engine afforded, the 11.5bhp single pot remained as an option. Despite its new engine the little Bond still could not match Reliant's overall top-speed performance, and the car that Sharps had hoped would compete head-on with the Tamworth product was reduced to flagging sales.

Recognizing that the Bond Minicar quite simply was outdated, and that customers wanting out and out economy vehicles were queuing to buy the Regal 3/25, Sharps took the desperate

The Mark G Bond featured a more commodious body than was fitted to the Mark E or F. Bond engineers achieved this by moving the windscreen forwards and devising a cut-back rear window in similar fashion to that of the Ford Anglia of the period. (National Motor Museum)

action of introducing a trimmed-down version of the single-cylinder 250G (albeit with an external opening boot at last). Sales of this no-frills Minicar were also minimal and in 1966 fifteen years of non-stop production of Bond Minicars came to an end. During this time, 26,000 vehicles had been built, but Reliant, throughout the same period, had produced at least double Bond's output.

A New Direction

Having introduced the media to an all-new Bond three-wheeler in the autumn of 1965, produc-

tion of the 875 did not begin until the summer of 1966. The latest Bond was an entirely different concept to the Minicar, and was targeted to rival the 3/25 Reliant head-on both in size and performance. Unlike earlier Bonds the 875 featured a glass-fibre body, and the engine, borrowed from the Hillman Imp, was positioned in the tail.

The 875 should have been Bond's three-wheeler masterpiece. It was, however, late going into production because of many technical problems, and the time that was lost only secured additional sales for Reliant. The Lake District's most notorious passes, the Wrynose and Hardknott, were chosen to test the 875 to its limit.

Elsewhere, the Bond was causing something of a stir – motoring journalists liked what they saw and were impressed by the prototype car's performance, not least when John Surtees squeezed 100mph out of the car at Brands Hatch. Much of Bond's problem was keeping the weight of the vehicle below 8cwt (406kg) in order to attract the lower tax threshold, and this meant changing some of the fundamental design features and using a detuned version of the Imp engine.

Meanwhile at Reliant . . .

In addition to having a completely revised body styling that was constructed entirely of glass fibre, under the skin the Reliant 3/25 boasted a new engine and several mechanical modifica-tions. Most significant was the all-alloy ohv engine that was designed and built by Reliant. Of lesser capacity than the Austin-inspired 17bhp 747cc side-valve unit, the new 598cc engine had an output of 24bhp. Chassis strengthening and revised front suspension – coil spring instead of torsion bar – were additional features, and improved methods of producing the glass-fibre bodywork and bonding it together helped to streamline car assembly. Never was an economy minicar more car-like, and customers approved the enhanced comfort and accommodation. Sales figures speak for themselves: during the period from 1963 to 1972 almost 106,000 vehicles were built; during the previous nine-year period output had been some 26,400 vehicles.

The Bond Mark G, in this instance the 250G, can be identified by its more angular air-intake. This car was pictured in 1993 at Huddersfield. (H. John Black)

When Reliant announced the Regal 3/25 for the 1963 model year, it was fitted with a new ohv 598cc light alloy engine that was designed and built by Reliant. There was revised styling too, and the reverse-rake rear window was seen on a number of cars including the Ford Classic and Citroën Ami 6, a derivative of the fabled 2CV. (Reliant)

The 3/25 found itself in the public gaze on a number of occasions. Not only did an early example provide support service for the three works-sponsored Sabre 4 sports cars during the 1963 Monte Carlo Rally, but the same car also embarked upon a proving run to the Sahara Desert totalling some 5,200 miles (8,370km), which it completed without any problem. Reliant 3/25s were used by a number of high-profile businesses, including the Automobile Association and BOAC.

When Reliant increased the 3/25's engine capacity to 700cc to yield an output of 29bhp in 1968, the model was redesignated Regal 3/30. By then, the slightly restyled Regal had been introduced in 1965 as an alternative to the existing model. Known as the 3/25 Super, the car featured styling by the Ogle design house and was given a slimmer and redefined nose. Introduced at the same price as the existing model, the standard car was now decreased in price by £18.

Possibly the one Reliant three-wheeler model that everyone remembers is the Robin. Making its debut in the autumn of 1973, the Ogle-designed Robin was deftly sculptured to produce a modern image; looking more like a 'normal' car, it featured a neatly trimmed interior and was given a hatch-type rear window which made handling luggage and shopping all the easier.

The Robin is the best known of all Reliant three-wheelers and has often been the subject of humour and derogation. For all this, the Robin has enjoyed healthy sales and a reputation for reliability and longevity. (Reliant)

The Robin can often be found undertaking a multitude of duties. In this instance this 1997 model serves a window cleaning business well.

Reliant Regal 3/25

Chassis
Type	Box section

Engine
Layout	Ohv four-cylinder in-line; water-cooled
Peak power	24.2bhp @ 3,000rpm
Bore × stroke	56×61mm
Cubic capacity	598cc
Compression ratio:	7.8:1

Transmission
Clutch	Single dry-plate clutch
Gearbox	Four-speed and reverse

Suspension
Front	Coil springs, leading arms and Girling dampers
Rear	Half-elliptic springs, Girling dampers

Brakes
Type	Girling hydraulic, drums all round

Tyres
Size	5.20×13in

Dimensions
Length	3,429mm (11ft 3in)
Width	1,448mm (4ft 9in)
Wheelbase	1,930mm (6ft 4in)
Track	1,168mm (3ft 10in)
Weight	8cwt (406kg)

Performance
Top speed	64mph (103km/h)
Fuel consumption	76mpg (3.72ltr/100km)

Reliant Robin

Chassis
Type	Steel frame with tubular cross members moulded into reinforced glass-fibre body

Engine
Layout	Ohv four-cylinder; water-cooled
Peak power	32bhp @ 5,500rpm
Bore × stroke	62.5×60.96mm
Cubic capacity	748cc

Transmission
Clutch	Single dry-plate clutch
Gearbox	Four-speed all-synchromesh

Suspension
Front	Leading arm to front wheel; heavy duty coil spring and telescopic damper
Rear	Long semi-elliptic single leaf springs

Steering
Type	Worm and peg

Brakes
Type	Hydraulically operated dampers all round

Tyres
Tyre size	5.20×10in
Wheel size	3½×10in

Dimensions
Length	2,565mm (8ft 5in)
Width	1,422mm (4ft 8in)
Wheelbase	2,159mm (7ft 1in)
Track	1,245mm (4ft 1in)
Weight	8cwt (406kg)

Performance
Top speed	72mph (116km/h)
Fuel consumption	45.2mpg (6.26ltr/100km)

Production modifications resulted in a more powerful Robin in 1975, thus pushing up the engine capacity to 850cc. When demand for the Robin began to falter in the late 1970s, Reliant devised a new body style and thus introduced the wedge-shaped Rialto. The new model was not particularly well received and it did little to boost flagging sales. Back came the faithful Robin together with further styling modifications, mostly to no avail simply because the little three-wheeler failed to lure away prospective customers who could buy a four-wheel car from Ford, Citroën, Peugeot or Fiat, to name but a few high-profile car makers, at considerably lower prices.

Bond is Dead

The Bond 875 had been in production for three years when Reliant, in February 1969, acquired

The 3/25 and Regal three-wheelers herald the Reliant model line-up, which includes the Scimitar sports cars, Kitten, Ant three-wheel commercials, and the company's heavy commercial model. (Reliant)

Bond Cars Ltd, Sharps Commercials having adopted that name in 1964. It comes as no surprise that Reliant, intent on maintaining the three-wheeler market for itself, decided that Bond production should cease.

The design of the Bond 875 is largely attributed to Lawrie Bond, who was persuaded to assist in the car's development. The shape of the 875 was much akin to that of the Reliant, and obviously Bond had hoped that the new three-wheeler, especially with its Hillman Imp engine, would attract sales away from Tamworth.

Despite the 875's attractive shape, weight-saving measures meant replacing the original seats with more basic types that were smaller, and the interior trim was pared down to the extent that even door panels were omitted. Apart from the windscreen, lighter-weight perspex was used instead of glass. To some, the 875 was therefore a disappointment.

The latest Robin engine is Reliant-made and has a capacity of 850cc. An all-alloy lightweight unit, the engine is used for a number of other applications, including being specified for use with certain kit cars and as a replacement for other types of engine. It is Reliant's claim that under specific circumstances their engine can achieve 100mpg (2.8ltr/100km). (Reliant)

Having been announced in the autumn of 1965, the Bond 875 eventually went into production in the spring of 1966. Unlike its forebears, the 875 featured a rear-positioned Hillman Imp engine that gave the car outstanding performance. In its style, the 875 would seem to have offered Reliant some serious competition which, in the event, failed to materialize. Those owners who bought the 875 were impressed with its performance, although the vehicle's interior finish left something to be desired. The model illustrated is the first of the series; later types had slightly revised styling to hint at a dummy front grille, while Mark II models were given an entirely new frontal design. (National Motor Museum)

Bond 875

Chassis

Type	Integral with reinforced glass-fibre body

Engine

Layout	Ohv four-cylinder in-line; water-cooled
Peak power	34bhp @ 4,700rpm
Bore × stroke	68 × 60mm
Cubic capacity	875cc
Compression ratio	8:1

Electrical

Battery	12V; 38amp/hr

Transmission

Clutch	Laycock diaphragm spring clutch
Gearbox	Four-speed all-synchromesh

Suspension

Front	Coil spring; telescopic dampers all round
Rear	Trailing arms with coil springs

Steering

Type	Burman worm and nut

Brakes

Type	Girling hydraulic drums

Tyres

Tyre size	Dunlop C41 tubeless 5.50 × 12in
Wheel size	Pressed steel, 4in rims

Capacity

Fuel tank	27ltr (6gal)

Dimensions

Length	2,946mm (9ft 8in)
Width	1,397mm (4ft 7in)
Wheelbase	1,980mm (6ft 6in)
Weight	880lb (400kg)

Performance

Top speed	80mph (130km/h)
Fuel consumption	34.5mpg (8ltr/100km)

Bond Cars did attempt to make improvements, and when the Mark II was introduced in March 1968 it featured a dummy front grille, new headlamps and a full-width bonnet. Even this was not sufficient to increase sales by any margin, and when Reliant took over the company in early 1969 one of the first directives was to scale down production. When assembly of the 875 finally ceased in 1970, production had been reduced to an average of four 875s a week.

In retrospect, the 875 potentially offered so much for relatively small investment. The car was poorly marketed which did little to boost sales. Had more time been spent on perfecting the design and curing some of the car's initial problems, it could have attracted many more customers. The reliable Hillman Imp engine did much to enhance the 875's performance, and during testing, acceleration and top speed, as well as smoothness of operation, were ably demonstrated.

Bond is Back

When Reliant unveiled its unique fun-type, wedge-shaped three-wheeler in 1970, it was the Bond name by which the car, which now has cult status, was known. The Bond Bug had arrived. Aimed at young and carefree motorists, the Bug certainly made its mark. To give some idea of the marketing aims of Reliant's directors, the Bug was viewed as being essentially at home on the beach. Considering the Bug's sparse apparel there is every reason to believe that the demand for such a vehicle would be limited, to say the least. But sell it did, probably because it was, at the time, so adventurous, especially in the sole colour scheme of Bug Tangerine, a hue then much in vogue for items as diverse as kitchens and motor cars.

The media loved the Bug. Even if some commentators viewed Reliant's Regal with some disdain, the fact that the Bug shared its stablemate's running gear and technology seemed not to matter. Available in three trim levels, the Bare Bug was very bare indeed and attracted only the most daring of customers. Much more substantial was the 700E, but it was the 700ES which,

Bond Bug	
Chassis	
Type	Welded box section; separate reinforced glass-fibre body
Engine	
Layout	Ohv four-cylinder in-line; water-cooled
Peak power	31bhp @ 3,000rpm
Bore × stroke	68 × 60mm
Cubic capacity	701cc
Transmission	
Clutch	Single dry-plate
Gearbox	Four-speed
Suspension	
Front	Coil spring leading arm
Rear	Coil springs and live axle with anti-roll bar
Shock absorbers	Girling telescopic all round
Steering	
Type	Burman-Douglas worm and peg
Brakes	
Type	Lockheed drums all round
Tyres	
Tyre size	5.20 × 10
Wheel size	$3\frac{1}{2}$J rim (F) 5J rim (R)
Capacity	
Fuel tank	23ltr (5gal)
Dimensions	
Length	2,750mm (9ft $\frac{1}{4}$in)
Width	1,430mm (4ft $8\frac{1}{4}$in)
Wheelbase	1,956mm (6ft 5in)
Weight	7.8cwt (396kg)
Performance	
Top speed	75.5mph (122km/h)
Fuel consumption	Touring: 51.7mpg (5.5ltr/100km); overall: 38mpg (7.5ltr/100km)

having sidescreens, heater and sun visor canopy offered the most appeal.

In October 1973 the Bug 750, fitted with the Robin 748cc engine, appeared, but this proved insufficient to revive flagging sales and production ended after 143 cars were built. Over three

One of the most controversial cars to be sold in Britain was the Bond Bug. Unique in 1970, it remains very much a cult vehicle over thirty years later. (Reliant)

decades later, however, the Bond Bug still cuts a dash on British roads and proves the point that the Tom Karen Ogle-designed microcar really was ahead of its time.

In the dawn of the third millennium, there was every reason to believe that the concept of the three-wheeler that both Bond and Reliant had promoted was consigned to history. Reliant ceased production of the Robin in 2000 when the company decided to import and market a range of microcars and vans built elsewhere. Some of these are described in a forthcoming chapter, but it is noteworthy that manufacture of

the three-wheel Robin resumed in 2002 following the agreement by Reliant to allow the car to be built under licence by B&N Plastics of Suffolk. As this book goes to press, production of the car is limited as vehicles are built to order, costing a little over £10,000. Two models are offered: the BN-1 has an all-new facia and console, sunroof and door trims; the BN-2 additionally features light reactive paint and electric windows. Modern techniques such as vacuum forming rather than injection moulding are employed in the making of the plastic components.

This Bug 700ES is centre of attention at a classic car meet. When the Bug was introduced Bond had been taken over by Reliant, and despite a certain amount of disparagement being aimed towards three-wheelers in general and Reliant in particular, the Bug was greeted with much acclaim and affection.

Bond Bugs were afforded minimal weather protection, the example illustrated here having the side screen in position.

The Robin 65 was a limited edition that was introduced to commemorate Reliant's sixty-fifth anniversary. Each car was painted metallic gold in colour and was comprehensively equipped with alloy wheels and a rear-screen wash/wipe system included in the specification. Note the Vauxhall Corsa headlamps and the modern styling arrangement. (Reliant)

Each Robin 65 was equipped with two-tone grey leather upholstery together with red carpets and trim. A plaque bearing the car's number and the original owner's name was fitted to each model. (Reliant)

Reliant ceased producing its familiar three-wheelers in 2000. Many commentators assumed it to be the end of the road for this most successful marque, especially as the concept was deemed to be outdated. Reliant continues to provide the chassis to an independent specialist, B&N Plastics of Suffolk, that produces under licence around ten vehicles a week, each costing from approximately £10,200. Two models are offered: the BN-1 has an all-new facia and console, sunroof and door trims; the BN-2 additionally features light-reactive paint and electric windows. (Reliant)

The new generation Reliant Robin Estate Car.

Bond Production		Reliant Production	
Mark A	1,973	Regal Mark I	1,000
Mark B	1,414	Regal Mark II	2,013
Mark C	6,399	Regal Mark III	2,798
Mark D	3,761	Regal Mark IV	1,298
Mark E	1,189	Regal Mark V	4,772
Mark F	6,493	Regal Mark VI	8,478
Mark G	3,250	Regal 3/25; 3/30	105,824
875, Mark I	2,038	Robin & Rialto	56,198
875, Mark II	1,043	Regent and	
Bug 700	2,127	Regal Vans	7,200 (includes pre-war
Bug 750	143		production)

4 Going to Work in an Egg

Popular belief is that the quintessential bubblecar emerged as a result of the Suez crisis and as a means of defying the draconian measures that petrol rationing had imposed. For many motorists wartime fuel rationing was anything but a distant memory, and when the Suez crisis erupted in 1956 they faced the prospect of forming long queues at those garages fortunate enough to have fuel reserves. The bubblecar, though, had been in existence for some three years.

Another accepted belief is that the bubblecar was invented by the Germans who, by the early to middle 1950s, were desperate to find cars that were cheap to run and, just as importantly, affordable to buy. The concept of the bubblecar was, however, established in Italy, home of arguably the best known of all minicars, the Fiat Topolino, the Little Mouse.

The quintessential bubblecar, the Isetta, which made its debut at the Turin motor show in 1953. The makers of what became known as the Little Egg, Iso of Milan, were more associated with refrigerators and motor scooters than motor cars, and therefore the sight of a tiny egg-shaped vehicle caused something of a sensation. The egg principle had already been established of course, when Frenchman Paul Arzens paraded his L'Oeuf Electrique around Paris during the war years. Iso's Little Egg was all the more practical in that it sported four wheels, had an enclosed cabin with comfortable accommodation for two adults and was powered by a minuscule two-stroke engine that offered extreme economy.

The design of the Isetta – Little Iso – is attributed to Ermenegildo Preti, a respected aeronautics engineer who, during the war, had worked on designs of gliders and radio-controlled flying bombs. After the war, Preti, who was born in 1918, lectured at the Milan Polytechnic, becoming professor of aeronautics; during the early 1950s he sought to design a revolutionary small car.

A New Concept

Ermenegildo Preti had decided that the most practical solution with regard to designing a minicar was to begin with few, if any, preconceived ideas. He was opposed to taking a medium or large car design and merely scaling it down. This had been done on a number of occasions and, in Preti's opinion, such results were not always entirely satisfactory. Preti sought to keep the vehicle's dimensions as small as possible, and he was convinced that one way of doing this was to do away with side doors. He succeeded in arriving at a design whereby the entire front panel of the car formed the sole door. By installing the engine over the rear wheels, passenger accommodation could be kept forwards as far as possible, and within an astonishingly short wheelbase, especially when front-wheel overhang was virtually eliminated. Preti was not alone in contesting the belief that having the engine and bonnet positioned ahead of the passengers afforded them complete protection in the event of an impact. Thus with an absence of bonnet and boot, an ovoid shape was realized that was both efficient and functional in use.

Preti put his ideas into practice by building a wooden model in the garage at his home. The potential difficulty lay in marketing his ideas, but

Built at Brighton, Sussex

Bubblecars were greeted with a huge amount of curiosity; in various forms they afforded enjoyable motoring to thousand of families worldwide and were economical to run. Reproduced here is publicity material for the Brighton-built Isetta.

when he approached Renzo Rivolta, the Milanese owner of Isotherm Refrigerators, Preti found a receptive ally. As it happened, Rivolta had enjoyed some initial success in building motor scooters, and going into business with a minimal motor car seemed a logical route to take.

Renzo Rivolta was not the only industrialist intent on building minicars. Fiat, too, was looking at various design proposals that were, essentially, grown-up motor scooters capable of providing car-like motoring at a minimum cost. In his autobiography, Dante Giacosa recalled evaluating design proposals in conjunction with helicopter designer Corradino D'Ascanio which were influenced by the Piaggio-built Vespa scooter. This was at the time when the Fiat 600, successor to the seemingly immortal Topolino, was in its development stage. Ultimately Giacosa decided on an altogether different route towards designing a minicar, more of which in a forthcoming chapter.

Development of the Isetta proceeded at Iso's Milan factory with the building of a prototype vehicle. Trials concluded that Preti's design was sound, although Rivolta insisted that a number of refinements be made. One of them concerned the chassis layout – employing a separate platform rather than a monocoque shell, Preti's provision of a single rear wheel was changed to a four-wheel configuration in the interests of stability and comfort. In order to keep costs to the absolute minimum, Preti, working alongside Iso's engineers, devised that the two rear wheels should have a track that was so narrow it would obviate the fitting of a differential. The cabin was judged to have an insufficient glazed area, and so was redesigned with larger windows. Perspex was specified for the side and rear windows, but for the door curved safety glass was used.

Among minicars of the time, the Isetta was unique. Overall length was 2,250mm (7ft 4$\frac{1}{2}$in), it had a wheelbase of 1,500mm (4ft 11in) and was 1,250mm (4ft 1$\frac{1}{2}$in) in its width and overall height. Despite the single front door, access to the interior proved to be relatively simple thanks to the steering column and wheel, which, being

---

Iso

Before the company began building bubblecars, Iso of Milan was respected for its motorcycles and motor scooters. When the Isetta failed to attract sufficient numbers of customers in its native Italy, Iso's senior director, Renzo Rivolta, licensed manufacturing to BMW in Germany, Velam in France, Borgward-Iso in Spain and Iso-Romi in Brazil. Iso later returned to car manufacturing when the company introduced the Rivolta in 1955, a sportscar having a top speed in excess of 140mph (225km/h). The Grifo followed in 1965 which, according to specification, was capable of almost 180mph (290km/h). A series of sportscars was introduced over successive years, each of limited production. In 1997 Iso returned to its minicar roots when Piero Rivolta, Renzo's son, who was by this time head of the company, introduced the Isigo, a 505cc microcar with a stainless-steel chassis.

---

attached to the inside of the door, moved with it courtesy of a universal joint. A rollback fabric roof was offered; it has been suggested, although not substantiated, that this was an obligation in order for the car's occupants to escape in the event of an accident.

Trials showed the Isetta to be extremely manoeuvrable and easy to park. An obvious advantage was the fact that the car could be parked nose-on to the pavement to facilitate easy and safe exit for the passengers. The Isetta's compact dimensions meant that parking nose-on took up far less road space than a conventional car, and its length really was not much greater than a full-size car's overall width. This was suitably exemplified by one of the motoring magazines sometime later when an Isetta was parked at right angles to a Bentley Mark Vl.

The engine first proposed for the Isetta was an air-cooled, two-stroke of 198cc, located on the right side of the car to balance the driver's weight. Within a year, the size of the engine had been increased to 236cc to provide maximum power of 9.5bhp at 4,500rpm. Transmission was effected via an all-synchromesh four-speed gearbox, with reverse, combined with the engine and duplex chain final drive.

The original Isetta was the product of Iso of Milan, a company that had much to do with motorcycles and scooters as well as domestic electrical appliances. This image records part of the Isetta build process at BMW. (BMW)

Iso Isetta	
Chassis	
Type	Separate frame with narrow-track rear axle
Engine	
Layout	Twin-cylinder; air-cooled
Peak power	9.5bhp @ 4,500rpm (4,750rpm with 198cc engine)
Bore×stroke	48×64.3mm (front piston);× 66mm (rear piston)
Cubic capacity	198cc (uprated to 236cc within a year)
Compression ratio	6.5:1
Transmission	
Clutch	Multi-plate, oil-immersed clutch
Gearbox	Four-speed
Suspension	
Front	Dubonnet-type; telescopic dampers, incorporated with springs
Rear	Telescopic dampers splay-mounted
Steering	
Type	Worm
Brakes	
Front	Hydraulic
Rear	One rear brake on solid rear axle
Tyres	
Tyre size	4.5×10in
Capacity	
Fuel tank	13ltr (2.9gal)
Dimensions	
Length	2,250mm (7ft 4½in)
Width	1,250mm (4ft 1½in)
Wheelbase	1,500mm (4ft 11in)
Weight	756lb (343kg)
Performance	
Top speed	44.9mph (72km/h)
Fuel consumption	50–60mpg (5.7–4.7ltr/100km)

Production of Iso's Isetta began in the autumn of 1953 with provision for fifty cars a day. Assembly of the Isetta was also scheduled to begin in Belgium in early 1954, and there were plans to build the car in Britain too, from 1955. Renzo Rivolta's plans were adventurous to say the least, and in addition to the European market, he envisaged selling the car in America. In the shadow of Rivolta's optimism there were, however, some problems. The price of the Isetta, which was equivalent to £300, was, for many Italians, simply too expensive, especially when a used Topolino could be acquired for a substantially lesser amount. Iso had made a claim that with increased production the price of the Isetta would be reduced. Fiat, however, was opposed to such an arrangement and took steps to prevent Iso out-pricing those cars that were considered to attract the same customer market share.

Italy Bursts the Bubble

Notwithstanding the Isetta's outstanding design and competent performance, Italian motorists failed to be attracted to it. Despite Iso's claim that its little bubble was a three-seater with luggage capacity – in fact, there was barely room for two adults and a child sitting three abreast, along with accommodation for shopping on the rear parcel shelf – only 6,000 Isettas were sold before the end of 1955. The Isetta did achieve some good publicity during the Mille Miglia races of 1954 and 1955, the unlikely competitors completing the 1,000-mile course and therefore taking first place in the index of performance. However, even media coverage as good as this proved to be insufficient to increase sales, and Iso found it difficult to maintain production.

For many Italian families Fiat's Topolino, small as it was, offered much more in the way of accommodation and interior space, despite some shortcomings and a relatively higher initial cost. Fiat had enjoyed the market leadership in ultra-small cars since 1936 and obviously the Turin empire was not going to relinquish its sales position without some sort of fight. This was achieved by way of publicity and influencing the

The Isetta underwent a number of design and styling modifications. Here, BMW Isettas can be seen outside the factory premises and depicted are two styling arrangements. Note the differences in the headlamps. (BMW)

motor trade, and the Isetta therefore looked doomed.

When Renzo Rivolta took the Isetta to the Geneva Motor Show in March 1954 it was not purely vehicle sales that he anticipated attracting. Selling the design of the Isetta was uppermost in his thoughts, and it was Geneva where he considered he had the best opportunity of finding a buyer. He was right, for he found a receptive ally in Eberhard Wolff, a long-standing senior design engineer with BMW.

BMW had, in the immediate post-war years, experienced severe difficulties. Its Eisenach factory was in Germany's eastern zone and the Munich works had been destroyed by bombing. The outlook was therefore bleak; production resumed at Eisenach, but it was 1948 before the Munich factory was able to recommence assembly, and then only for motorcycles. Car building

did not resume at Munich until 1952 when the 501 became available. There were those within BMW who considered that the company should develop a small utilitarian car, not only to cater for the demand in Germany and Western Europe, but also as a means of getting the factory into something approaching meaningful production.

BMW had, during the interwar years, gained experience building small cars when the company assembled the Austin Seven under licence. The arrangement lasted until 1932 when BMW sought to concentrate on larger and more expensive motor cars. Was the time right, post-war, to return to producing another small car? Obviously a number of directors considered so, and plans were drawn up to build a 600cc motorcycle-engined coupé that was to have been known as the 331. The surviving prototype indicates that

BMW

Before building motor cars, BMW enjoyed a long association with the aviation industry. The company's ancestry can be traced to 1916 when the Bavarian Aeroplane Works (Bayerische Flugzeugwerke) was established, the name changing in 1917 to Bayerische Motoren Werke. Camillo Castiglione and Franz-Joseph Popp were the principal decision-makers within the organization, and it was their influence that directed BMW into building engines for motorcycles and commercial vehicles.

After World War I BMW had been forbidden to make aero engines, and so in 1923 it introduced its first motorcycle, displaying features that became synonymous with the marque, such as horizontally opposed cylinders and shaft drive.

In 1928 BMW acquired the Eisenach firm Dixi Werke, makers of three models of motor car, including the Austin Seven which it built under licence. It was the baby Austin that BMW retained, abandoning production of the two other Dixi models, and from early 1929 they were badged as BMWs. The Austins remained in production until 1932, although in the meantime BMW had introduced some styling changes. After 1932 BMW introduced its own models. The first of these was the 3/20 which was joined in 1933 by the Type 303; in 1936 the company's first four-door saloon was introduced, but it was the 328 that was recognized for its aesthetic styling and sporting potential.

BMW built the Isetta and the larger 600 model as a means of recovery during the austerity years. In the ensuing decades BMW has been noted for its engineering qualities, and from January 2003 the company will produce Rolls-Royce motor cars, having acquired the Rolls-Royce name.

this would have been an elegant machine that was, essentially, a scaled-down 501. BMW directors Hans Grewenig, Fritz Fiedler and Kurt Donath nevertheless had the final say on the matter and ultimately scrapped the plan as they were convinced that such a car would be too expensive to develop and that it would possibly undermine the company's image.

Eberhard Wolff discovered the Isetta at the 1954 Geneva Motor Show and was clearly impressed by its clever design. Wolff was one of those who had anticipated that BMW should produce a minicar, but one with more sophisticated engineering than some of the fragile-looking machines that had found their way on to the market.

Being totally different to anything that he had previously seen, Wolff made a brief but meticulous survey of the car. With its separate chassis and space-saving features, Wolff deemed that this was the car that BMW should be building. Wolff's urgent call to BMW headquarters was sufficient to summon the interest of those directors who were previously opposed to producing a minicar, and this alone gives rise to the belief that Wolff had been sent to Geneva primarily to establish some ideas as to what direction BMW should take in returning to profitable business.

Wolff succeeded in convincing his directors that here was a design that needed very little in the way of development, and one that could be put into production with the minimum of outlay and time because Rivolta was ready to supply body presses as part of the licensing agreement. Seeing the Isetta for themselves, Grewenig, Fiedler and Donath were also satisfied that this was the correct route to take, although their final decision might not have been entirely based on Wolff's perceptions. With the Fuldamobil and the Messerschmitt having already made their appearance in Germany and attracting increasing numbers of customers, BMW's directors now accepted that the time was right to introduce the Isetta into the country.

BMW did, however, have some misgivings concerning some of the Isetta's design features, and before any commitment could be made, the Munich firm insisted that some relatively minor changes be undertaken. Rivolta put up no objections to this, being only too pleased to complete contractual arrangements.

A Blatant Copy

Eberhard Wolff was right in his perception that Iso's little egg on wheels would appeal to other German manufacturers. There were two other players – Ernst Heinkel, the aeroplane designer

An early Isetta production line. When the single door was opened the steering assembly moved accordingly, the swivelling device being clearly apparent here. Note also the car's window arrangement, the sunroof and spare wheel. (BMW)

whose aircraft had helped to spearhead the Luft-waffe, and the bicycle maker Jakob Hoffmann who built Vespa motor scooters under licence. The Heinkel story will be told elsewhere in this chapter, so first we will look at Hoffmann and his Auto Kabine.

Together with his designer Hans Roger, Hoffmann had devised his Isetta look-alike following a failed approach to Renzo Rivolta to build the little Iso under licence. Rivolta had turned down Hoffmann's proposal because, in his opinion, Hoffmann, despite having experience assembling Vespa scooters, was not equipped with sufficient manufacturing or financial resources to undertake the project. Hoffmann therefore decided to build his own version of the Isetta, but with pertinent differences.

In concept, Hans Roger's styling of the Hoffmann Kabine was so much like that of the Isetta's it could, at first glance, be mistaken for it. However, instead of adopting the Isetta's single front opening door, the Hoffmann featured a side door, which was on the passenger side of the vehicle. There was little difference in the chassis arrangement between the two cars, both having twin rear wheels to aid stability but with such a narrow track that there was no need for a differential. The Auto Kabine did, however, feature a brace under the passenger area to provide additional strengthening, and Hoffmann chose to use a 250cc air-cooled horizontally opposed motorcycle engine that was of his own design.

The development of the Hoffmann was carried out at the time that BMW was negotiating an agreement with Iso, and there is every reason to believe that it was Hoffman's aim to launch his Auto Kabine ahead of the BMW Isetta. However, when Hoffmann unveiled his bubble in June 1954 the car did not meet with the anticipated applause. Commentators, knowing that BMW had been working closely with Iso on their bubblecar project, were understandably confused as to whether or not Hoffmann had beaten BMW into reaching an agreement. When Hoffmann tried to secure finances with which to tool up for production, he found that there wasn't a bank that would

work with him, and it quickly became apparent that BMW had engaged in legal action to prevent him producing the car.

Forced out of business in early 1955, Hoffmann had produced only 113 Auto Kabines. The failure of Hoffmann's enterprise nevertheless brought the Isetta and BMW into the forefront of media attention, and the publicity ultimately worked to BMW's advantage. For bubblecar enthusiasts the Hoffmann Auto Kabine represents the Holy Grail; it is unsure whether any examples have survived, and if they have they must surely be of some considerable value, if only in terms of curiosity.

Ernst Heinkel's Bubble

When the Isetta came into prominence in 1953, Ernst Heinkel's motor-scooter business was already well established, building the Tourist machine which was powered by a single-cylinder, four-stroke engine of 150cc capacity. Anticipating a need for small air-cooled petrol engines, Heinkel produced a number of designs suitable for varied applications, one being to power a small commercial vehicle. Sharing similar practice to that of the Bond Minicar, the Tempo mini truck as built by Vidal & Sohn used a Heinkel single-cylinder, two-stroke engine that was mounted above the single front wheel and driving it via a chain mechanism. Heinkel, of course, was a familiar name throughout the world, and was synonymous with aviation and jet propulsion. Ernst Heinkel was also associated with Saab, and in 1951 was responsible for devising a three-cylinder, two-stroke engine for the Swedish company.

Like so many European aircraft makers Heinkel found it necessary to diversify into other activities after the war, and automobile manufacturing, especially for the mass market, appealed. The emergence of the Isetta had prompted Heinkel to study the Italian design, and with his aeronautical experience he arrived at some different conclusions to that of Ermenegildo Preti. He regarded the Isetta as being over-engineered and believed that the design principles could be better utilized to reduce the car's weight and make improved use of the limited resources that were then available.

Heinkel's aviation experience led him to believe that it was unnecessary to employ a separate chassis and that a monocoque design would allow lower build costs as well as improving the car's aerodynamics. Heinkel, of course, contemplated using an engine of his own design, initially 174cc, and he envisaged his car as having a single rear wheel instead of two. The designer also sought to improve on accommodation by affording sufficient space for two adults and a child on the bench seat, with additional space behind for another child and some luggage, although there was not a proper rear seat.

Heinkel was developing his Kabinen or Cabin Scooter at the same time as Hoffmann was working on the Auto Kabine and BMW was continuing negotiations to build the Isetta under licence. In 1954 Heinkel unveiled his prototype machine, which at first glance appreared to share many similarities with the Isetta. It did, however, have a more prominent nose, and the tail was more rounded to incorporate the engine. Of particular interest is that the design was seen to have a lower centre of gravity courtesy of the chassis-less construction, and the perspex dome was marginally larger than that of the Isetta's.

On subsequent designs, Heinkel found it necessary to divorce the drive train from within the cabin structure and instead contain it under the

Two other manufacturers built bubblecars in the general form of the Isetta. One was Jakob Hoffmann, the other Ernst Heinkel. Only a few Hoffmanns were built before production was abandoned, but the Heinkel found many customers. Depicted here is an example of a Trojan-built Heinkel.

Unlike the Isetta, which had a separate chassis, the Heinkel was built using an integral chassis. The prototype Heinkel was shown in 1954 but production did not begin until 1956, largely as a result of discussions with BMW. The vehicle seen in this photograph is an early Trojan-built Heinkel.

In addition to the saloon, the Heinkel was built as a van. Note the rear-opening hatch.

Ernst Heinkel, 1888–1958

As an engineering student in the early years of the twentieth century, Ernst Heinkel became an ardent advocate of powered flight and, in 1911, built and flew his own design of box kite. As a designer, Heinkel quickly acquired a high reputation and was courted by Hansa-Brandenburg. The financier Camillo Castiglioni wanted Heinkel to work for him, and the only way he could be sure to attract the young engineer was to buy out Hansa-Brandenburg. This led to the introduction of a series of successful seaplanes that were used to secure Germany's coastal defences during World War I.

Heinkel established his own business in 1922 and produced a number of military aircraft, the He-25 earning for itself a particular status, along with the H.D. 43 fighter biplane. In 1939 Heinkel built the world's first jet aircraft, the He178. Having to diversify into auto engineering after World War II, Heinkel nevertheless returned to aircraft building when restrictions on German armaments were lifted.

Ernst Heinkel was one of the top four German aircraft designers during the interwar period, and on his death he left to the world a formidable engineering legacy.

distinct notch at the rear. This also had the effect of increasing the cabin area in addition to aiding the vehicle's stability by increasing the wheelbase. The window configuration was also similar to that of the Isetta, and the Heinkel, too, featured a single door at the front. Unlike the Isetta where the steering wheel hinged forwards as the door opened, that on the Heinkel remained static.

While the Hoffmann design was deemed to be a blatant copy of the Isetta, there was no such dilemma when it came to evaluating the Heinkel. There were some very good reasons for this, despite the fact that the two machines certainly looked very similar. Heinkel was a highly respected engineer who attracted more credibility than Hoffmann; his business was on a much more established footing; and underneath the bubblecar's exterior there were some fundamental differences between the two designs.

That BMW and Heinkel were involved in discussions about their respective cars there is no

doubt. The introduction of the BMW Isetta was ahead of schedule compared with Heinkel's Kabinen, and Heinkel agreed that the debut of his product be delayed until early 1956. Heinkel appears not to have been too concerned about the delay, as he was having difficulty finding suitable premises in which to build his car, as his other factories were working at full capacity building engines and motor scooters. Ultimately, premises on an airfield at Speyer were purchased, which gives rise to the theory that Heinkel was waiting until the ban of German armaments was lifted before resuming aircraft production. The financial cost of installing car-manufacturing equipment meant that Heinkel had resources only to install welding jigs and a paint booth, and that provision for body panel presses would have to follow. Heinkel's problems were overcome when the Hamburg firm of Vidal & Sohn, with whom he enjoyed a good working relationship, agreed to supply the Kabinen's body panels.

BMW Launches the Isetta

Before putting the Isetta into production BMW's engineers introduced a number of changes to the car's original specification. Instead of using the engine that Iso had specified, BMW had insisted on fitting its own engine, a derivative of the single-cylinder, four-stroke R25 245cc motorcycle unit. In BMW's opinion this would not only be attractive to German customers but would also afford increased power, raising the bhp from nine to twelve, in addition to being all the more reliable. Contemporary road tests conducted by the leading motoring journals indicated that the Iso's sturdy engine was the least attractive feature of the vehicle because of its lack of smoothness at low revs. At the same time, BMW undertook to redesign the gearbox to the company's exacting standards. BMW engineers also paid attention to the Isetta's suspension by increasing the travel of the front springs by 50mm (2in) to provide a softer ride.

BMW had also expressed concern about the design of headlamps that were used for the Isetta. Replacement pod-type lamps that were housed

(Above) *The front view of the Messerschmitt is unmistakeable with its bug-eye headlamps and transparent dome. The narrowness of the passenger cabin is apparent. Note the side lamps on the wing tops, and the position of the front direction indicators. The Messerschmitt badge is of interest: when production was taken over by FMR an emblem incorporating three diamonds was adopted.*

(Right) *The Kabinenroller's dome is hinged along the right-hand side of the vehicle to permit access to the passenger compartment. In those countries where vehicles drive on the left, care has to be taken entering and exiting because the cabin roof tilts into the path of overtaking traffic. Where traffic drives on the right, passengers enter and leave the Messerschmitt from the road rather than the pavement.*

(Above) *The KR175 interior showing the handlebar steering, controls and instrumentation. The rear passenger sits with their legs stretched out alongside the driver's seat. Ventilation in the cabin is restricted, which means that travelling over long distances in high temperatures can be uncomfortable.*

(Below) *The Messerschmitt's right-hand gear lever has fore-and-aft movement; neutral is selected by use of the trigger. To select reverse, the engine is stopped and then re-started by depressing and turning the ignition key. With the engine running in reverse, the gears can be used as for forward motion.*

(Below) *The rear cover opens to reveal the Messerschmitt's powerplant, in this instance a Sachs 174cc engine. Final drive, fuel tank and spare wheel are all visible.*

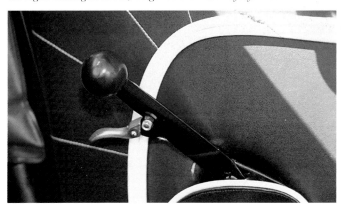

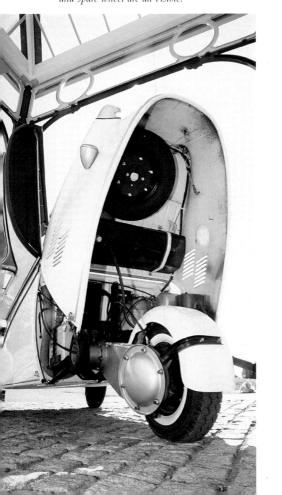

(Below) *When viewed from the side the aerodynamic shape of the Messerschmitt can be appreciated to good effect. The minimal space within the passenger cabin in which to accommodate baggage meant fitting an external luggage rack.*

(Above) *Isetta Bubblecar styling was extensively employed in the design of the BMW 600. The front-opening door gives access to the front compartment while a kerb-side door affords access to the rear seats.*

(Below) *Despite its tiny proportions, the BMW 600 is a genuine four-seater with generous interior accommodation. Suspension is surprisingly compliant, and the vehicle is capable of transporting a full complement of passengers over long distances in comfort.*

(Below) *When the front door of the 600 is opened, the steering column swivels to allow unhindered access to the car's front seat. The central gear lever is visible, and note how the instrument binnacle is incorporated into the door assembly.*

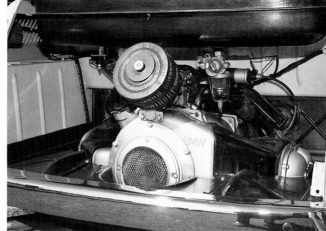

(Above) *The BMW 600's engine compartment showing the 582cc flat-twin engine.*

(Above) *The capacious interior of the BMW 600. Controls for choke, heater and fuel reserve are to the driver's left; the stalk for the dipping and flashing of headlamps is on the left of the steering column, and that for the horn and direction indicators is on the right. To the left of the instrument binnacle is the headlamp on/off switch, and to its right are the windscreen wiper and ignition and starter controls.*

(Above) *The Scootacar emblem.*

(Left) *Scootacars were built by the Hunslet Engine Company of Leeds, the styling having been devised by Henry Brown who had previously designed the Rodley car. The fibreglass body was constructed in two halves, the join being in the middle of the front and rear panels and along the roof.*

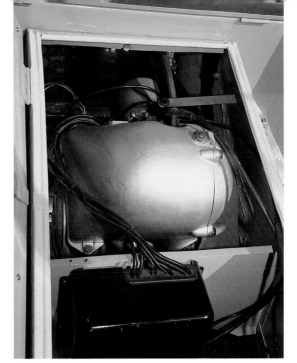

(Above) *Despite its pear-like shape the Mark 1 Scootacar possesses good stability and handling characteristics. It has a Villiers 9E 197cc two-stroke engine (right) located under the driver's seat, which had to be removed to gain access to it. As might be expected, performance is somewhat tardy.*

(Below) *A single door on the left-hand side of the Scootacar provides access to its interior. The ultra-compact dimensions, the tiny wheels, the exposed spare wheel mounted at the rear and the high-level indicators all played their part in ensuring the car was produced in only limited numbers.*

(Above and below) *The Scootacar's controls and instrumentation; the red lever above the speedometer is the headlamp flasher. Note the handlebar steering.*

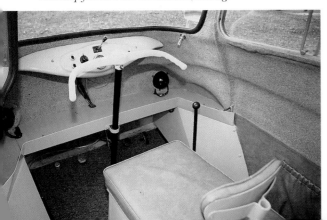

The Heinkel made its debut soon after BMW had arranged to take over the building of Isettas from Iso of Italy. Originally produced in Germany, Heinkels were subsequently built in Eire by Dundalk Engineering, in Argentina, and in Britain under licence by Trojan at Croydon. In a style similar to that of the Isetta, Heinkels and Trojans have a single front-opening door.

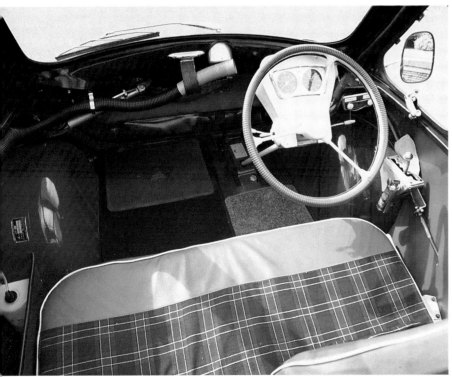

The Trojan's interior, showing the driving position and the gear selector. Unlike the Isetta's swivelling steering column, the Trojan's is rigid. Because the door is not reverse-hinged for right-hand drive cars, entry and exit to and from the vehicle make for an interesting diversion

(Right) *The Trojan 200 with its 198cc single-cylinder four-stroke engine was available with left- or right-hand drive. Microcar enthusiasts admire Heinkels and Trojans for their free-running engines, reliability and overall performance.*

(Below) *Ernst Heinkel chose to design his car with an integral chassis to reduce weight and production costs. The vehicle was originally specified as a four-wheeler, the rear wheels being set close together to avoid the need to fit a differential. The three-wheeled Trojan 200, as seen here, was introduced to benefit from lower rates of taxation. The cabin glass configuration remained the same throughout production.*

(Below) *When BMW took over production of the Isetta, the Bavarian company gradually introduced a number of styling changes to include full-length side windows.*

(Below) *A detachable panel reveals the BMW 298cc single-cylinder ohv engine. When the Isetta was road-tested by* The Motor, *highly creditable performance figures were revealed.*

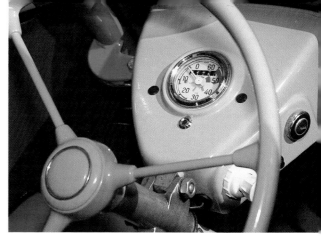

(Above) *Isettas had minimal instrumentation. The binnacle provides for speedometer and distance recorder, dynamo charge indicator, direction indicator warning light and headlamp main beam tell-tale. To the right is the ignition and starter switch.*

(Above) *That this is a late-model Isetta is shown by the style of headlamps, previous types having been set within nacelles along the sides of the car.*

(Right) *The Isetta's door opens sufficiently wide to afford easy access and exit to and from the cabin interior. The swivelling steering column is an aspect of the car's design that owners find particularly favourable. Parking the Isetta at right angles facing the kerb was a marketing feature of the car.*

(Right) *Sliding windows and an opening fabric roof allow adequate ventilation to the Isetta's interior.*

in tapering nacelles and mounted at a higher position than previously provided considerably improved illumination. Flashing direction indicators were repositioned from the top of the headlamps to the car's flanks so that they were equidistant between the front and rear of the vehicle, thereby doing away with the need for repeater lamps in the tail. Possibly the most obvious design change was, mechanically, the least significant – the adoption of the BMW logo on the door, beneath the windscreen.

The BMW Isetta was launched in the spring of 1955 to much acclaim. Never appreciated by German motorists when sold by Iso, the Isetta instantly appealed and within the first year of manufacturing some 10,000 bubbles were sold. The following year was even better news for BMW, with sales exceeding 22,500 vehicles.

Assured of the Isetta's success, BMW, after having evaluated sales throughout the first year, introduced further styling changes. The tapered headlamp nacelles were replaced by a more compact design, and the indicators, which were vertical teardrops, gave way to horizontal rectangular units. The quarter bumpers of the early model were abandoned in favour of a full-width bumper positioned along the bottom of the door. Items such as the door handle and wheel trims, which were left over from the Iso, were also restyled along with the rear number-plate housing. The engine compartment cover was also redesigned with louvres to aid cooling.

BMW, confident that the Isetta would appeal to those customers wanting affordable motoring as well as those fortunate enough to have a second car, introduced some external styling

A line-up of Isettas at the BMW factory. These cars have the later type of headlamps, which afforded better illumination than the earlier nacelle type. (BMW)

BMW took over production of the Isetta in 1955. This scene shows an element of the construction process soon after BMW's acquisition of the bubblecar. (BMW)

BMW Isetta

Chassis

Type	Box section and tubular frame

Engine

Layout	Single-cylinder; air-cooled
Peak power	12bhp @ 5,800rpm
Bore × stroke	68×68mm
Cubic capacity	245cc

Electrical

Battery	12V

Transmission

Clutch	Single dry-plate clutch
Gearbox	Four-speed constant mesh gearbox in unit with engine

Suspension

Front	Dubonnet-type independent incorporating helical springs and hydraulic dampers
Rear	Quarter-elliptic springs and telescopic dampers

Brakes

Type	Hydraulic drum

Dimensions

Length	2,286mm (7ft 6in)
Width	1,378mm (4ft $6\frac{1}{4}$in)
Wheelbase	1,473mm (4ft 10in)
Track	Front: 1,207mm (3ft $11\frac{1}{2}$in); rear: 521mm (1ft $8\frac{1}{2}$in)
Weight	7cwt (356 kg)

Performance

Top speed	55.5mph (89km/h)
Fuel consumption	62mpg (4.7ltr/100km)

options such as additional aluminium trim mouldings and the availability of two-tone paint schemes. For all models, though, there was a significant safety modification, with safety glass replacing the plexiglass side windows. For customers who needed to carry more baggage than the Isetta could accommodate within the passenger cabin, external luggage racks provided a solution. BMW did also introduce a bolt-on platform that could be fitted in place of the rear window, an accessory that really was not capable of taking anything of great weight and which severely restricted rearward vision from within the cabin.

Van conversions also became available, but these were supplied through the respected coach-building firm Buhne of Berlin. Buhne had, before the war, produced coachwork for BMW, Mercedes and Rolls-Royce among others, and in post-war years specialized in the conversion of police cars and post office vehicles. The Buhne conversion for Isettas was clearly aimed at the small-business market, although there is little evidence that anything more than a few examples were built.

More Styling Changes

For 1957, BMW introduced some far-reaching styling changes that significantly altered the profile of the Isetta. In place of the familiar six-light configuration, BMW adopted full-length side windows with sliding glasses along with a modified rear window. Arguably less fussy than the previous design, the new model nevertheless lost some of its curvaceousness, albeit the improvements to ventilation were welcome. Improvements to the car's interior styling resulted in there being increased luggage accommodation, achieved by lowering the rear parcel shelf. A convertible model also became available, with a hood replacing the rear window.

The changes had at first been applied to export models, which also received a more powerful version of the R25 engine. In place of the 245cc unit was a 295cc engine that developed 13bhp at 6,000rpm, and those cars to which it was fitted became known as the Isetta 300. Further techni-

cal modifications were made to the suspension system, which markedly improved the car's ride. This entailed changing the chassis layout slightly by fitting longer quarter elliptic springs on the rear axle, but it was at the front that most attention was paid. Long and vertical coil springs enclosing double-acting hydraulic dampers replaced the previous Dubonnet arrangement, although the wheels continued to be carried on rear-hinged fore and aft swinging arms. There had been some criticism concerning the pitching motion that was experienced with the Isetta, especially when braking harshly and driving over less than smooth surfaces; the revised technology provided some 32 per cent increase in wheel travel to afford a softer ride than previously.

The styling modifications that heralded the 300 model are those that most people recognize when referring to the Isetta. It was not solely the home market that BMW was keen to exploit, and the Isetta quickly became a familiar sight throughout Europe and further afield. In Britain, too, the bubblecar craze existed and Isettas were built under licence at Brighton in an abandoned railway workshop.

Heinkel Competes with BMW

When it made its debut in March 1956, Heinkel's design was perceived as being almost identical to that of the Isetta. It, too, had a single door that formed the complete front of the car, but unlike the Isetta the fixed steering column marginally impeded entering and exiting the car. *Top Gear* magazine, when evaluating it alongside the Isetta, made the claim the cars were 'Two of a Kind', although in fact there were distinct differences.

Despite its smallness, the Heinkel offered a greater amount of space within the cabin, which was achieved by having a rear seat that was suitable only for young children or for carrying luggage. Unlike the Isetta, the Heinkel's front seat folded to allow access to the rear, and exactly how easy or difficult it was to manoeuvre across the car's interior can be left to one's imagination. Getting into and out of an Isetta was facilitated by having the swivelling mechanism built into

The Isetta was significantly restyled for the 1957 model year, and the modifications can be seen in this assembly picture. Instead of a six-light configuration the vehicle was given full-length side windows with sliding glasses. Other revisions applied to the suspension, to afford a softer ride, and increased power courtesy of a 295cc engine. In the background can be seen the BMW 700 production line, which dates this photograph to some time after 1959. (BMW)

the steering column, something which could have been an advantage on the Heinkel had it not been for possible infringement of patents.

On the road, the Heinkel's relatively soft suspension soaked up uneven surfaces and cobblestones with ease compared to the Isetta's firmer ride. Nevertheless, contemporary road tests warned that severely rough surfaces should be avoided at all costs, something that wasn't always easy, especially in more rural locations. Behind the wheel, the Heinkel's steering tended to be less precise than that of the Isetta. The gear selection mechanism was quite different on both

cars, the Isetta having a conventional gear change but with a completely reversed layout to that of a normal car, the lever being mounted on the side of the body. That of the Heinkel had more of motorcycle practice about it and was of the quadrant type. Having selected first gear, the lever had merely to be pushed forwards, notch by notch, as the speed of the car increased, and it was possible to achieve some very rapid changes.

The Suez crisis was at its height when the Heinkel was introduced, and the effects of petrol rationing were sufficient to put the car in the

Heinkels offered more interior space and softer suspension than Isettas. Trojan was keen to emphasize the car's manoeuvrability, which is depicted in this specially processed publicity picture.

limelight immediately. Heinkel's claim of a frugal 94mpg (3ltr/100km) fuel consumption was music to the ears of fuel-starved motorists, but in reality such extraordinary running was seldom achieved. The best that *Autocar* could attain was 85mpg (3.3ltr/100km), and mostly under general driving conditions it was not possible to better 65mpg (4.4ltr/100km).

Designated Model 150, the 174cc Heinkels were noted for their free-running engines, and today enthusiasts regard this model as being the finest that the company built. Compared to the new-look Isetta with its sliding side windows, Heinkels featured more of the essential 'bubble profile', which was typified by the car's more rounded shape, and which was derived from having a chassis-less construction.

The British concessionaire for Heinkel was Peter Nobel of Noble Motors (note the spellings!), who became associated with the Fuldamobil and the eventual appearance of the Nobel 200. Nobel was never slow to miss a sales or publicity opportunity, and on one occasion he made headline news when he encouraged at least five attractive young women to squeeze inside one of his Heinkels. The fact that the glamour actress Sabrina was on hand to offer a helping hand did wonders for the marketing stunt, and no doubt readers of the popular press were suitably impressed.

Heinkel 150

Chassis
Type   Integral

Engine
Layout   Single-cylinder; air-cooled
Bore × stroke   60 × 61mm
Cubic capacity   174cc
Compression ratio   7.4:1

Transmission
Clutch   Wet multi-plate clutch
Gearbox   Four-speed with reverse

Suspension
Front   Independent
Rear   Trailing arms

Steering
Type   Rack and pinion

Dimensions
Length   2,654mm (8ft 8½in)
Width   1,359mm (4ft 5½in)
Wheelbase   1,746mm (5ft 8¾in)
Weight   535lb (243kg)

Performance
Top speed   50mph (80km/h)
Fuel consumption   65mpg (4.4ltr/100km);
                        touring: 85mpg (3.3ltr/100km)

In October 1956 Heinkel introduced two new models, the 153 and 154. Externally, the cars were nearly identical to the 150, albeit the 154 was designed as a four-wheeler with the rear wheels set close together. As with the Isetta, the four-wheel Heinkel had no need for a differential. Both the 153 (having three wheels) and 154 were fitted with a 204cc engine which gave a welcome boost to power over the 150 model. Within six months the size of the engine was marginally reduced to 198cc in order to comply with tax concessions in those countries having a tax break for cars under 200cc. In Britain, of course, three-wheelers enjoyed a tax advantage, and therefore the 154 did not sell in any significant numbers.

Heinkels imported to Britain by Noble Motors were brought in by air, and not, as might have been thought, by sea. They were loaded into Dakotas, five at a time, and flown from Hanover to a distribution point in Croydon where, ironically, the cars were later assembled by the Trojan company. The effects of petrol rationing meant that demand for bubblecars and the like increased so much that Noble Motors secured all of Heinkel's European delivery solely for the UK throughout the Suez crisis.

Heinkels were built in Britain at Purley Way in Croydon, Surrey, by the Trojan company. Note the large Trojan emblem on the door, its size being necessary to cover the holes made for the Heinkel badge.

Irish Heinkels and the Trojan

Ernst Heinkel had always intended returning to aircraft manufacturing when the ban on aero production that was imposed on Federal Germany at the end of World War II was lifted. This eventually occurred in 1957, and immediately Heinkel sought to secure NATO contracts. Wishing to dispose of his bubblecar business after having built some 6,000 vehicles (total production was 6,436), interested parties were invited to bid for Heinkel production under licence. Two companies, one in Eire and the other in Argentina, took over assembly. South America also became home to Iso's Isetta, in that it was built under licence by Romi-Isetta of Brazil after production had ceased in Italy.

Heinkel's were built in the Irish Republic by Dundalk Engineering between 1958 and 1962. They carried the Heinkel name but with the letter I (signifying Heinkel-Ireland), following the by now familiar Flying H emblem. Whilst complete cars were assembled in Ireland, the engines continued to be built and supplied by Heinkel in Germany. There have been claims that production of the Irish Heinkels was beset with problems, not least that the build quality often fell somewhat short of what was expected. In fairness, a fair quantity of the Dundalk cars have survived, so tales of poorly finished vehicles cannot be entirely substantiated.

The period in which Heinkels were built in Ireland also saw the introduction of the Mini in 1959. The arrival of the Mini was responsible for changing much of the minicar scene in Britain and Europe. For out and out economy, however, there were very few cars that could outdo the Heinkel. For absolute cheekiness, nothing could compete with Heinkel-Ireland's convertible model, which, with its hood down, appeared more like a scooter than a car. With its hood raised, the vehicle retained much of the saloon's charm and cosiness.

Those Heinkels built in Argentina were of the four-wheel variety and were assembled over a period of three years. They differed from their European cousins in that the harsh local environment called for modifications to the engine. The dusty roads meant that the original type of air filter was inadequate, and the type used on the Volkswagen Beetle was employed, although it was necessary to adapt the engine cover, resulting in compromised access to the motor.

With the concept of the bubblecar in decline, Dundalk Engineering sold the rights to build the Heinkel in 1962 to Trojan of Purley Way, Croydon in Surrey. Possibly bubblecars were a far cry from the Trojan name that was familiar at the time, especially in respect of commercial vehicles that were part of the everyday scene on British roads. It was Peter Agg who was responsible for negotiating the Heinkel deal – he had purchased Trojan in 1959, having been British distributor for Lambretta scooters since 1950. Renamed Trojans, these British-built Heinkels were adapted to right-hand drive, the modification being not entirely satisfactory since the door remained hinged as previously, thus making entry and exit that much more difficult.

Outwardly identical to the German and Irish models, Trojans were nevertheless easily identified by the large Trojan badge on the door. The cars were assembled in Croydon; the basic cage of the car was formed out of 38mm (1.5in) diameter tubes using the argon arc process, after

---

The Original Trojan

'Can you afford to walk?' was the Trojan slogan. Trojans were designed by Leslie Hounsfield (1877–1957), and were generally recognized for their rugged construction and dependability, both factors that gave the marque a loyal and dedicated following. When introduced, the Trojan Utility Car cost £230 and was built by Leyland Motors of Kingston in Surrey. Keen to be associated with with the vehicle, Leyland decided to market it alongside its considerably more luxurious car, the Leyland Eight. The arrangement did not last, and Trojan began to rely on sales of its commercial vehicles. After 1930, a new range of models was introduced that were designed to compete with the smaller Standards and Singers. The Trojan is most readily remembered for its postwar commercials carrying decals for some of Britain's most popular foods.

Trojans were built in two versions. Three-wheelers were available in the UK and other markets in order to comply with taxation restrictions; four-wheelers – the rear wheels were set close together to avoid use of a differential – were sold elsewhere. In this publicity photograph it is a case of 'his and hers'.

which body panels were stamped out in 24-gauge steel and then spot-welded in jigs. Produced in two halves, top and bottom, which were then welded together, any imperfections were filled with lead and then sanded down before being dipped in rust inhibitor and then painted.

A fair number of locally sourced components were used in the building of the Trojan: shock absorbers were supplied by Armstrong; latches and hinges by Wilmot Breedon; and headlamps by Miller. Trojan built two versions of the Heinkel: a four-wheel model for those markets where there were no restrictions apart from engine capacity in respect of taxation; and a three-wheel model – the 200 – for the British market. A van version of the Trojan was

contemplated, but although at least several examples were built, it appears that the project was abandoned before going into full-scale production.

For the same reason that market forces had been responsible for declining sales of the Dundalk-built Heinkels, sales of the Trojan began seriously to wither in the mid-1960s. Production continued at the rate of a few cars a week until early 1965. However, engine production remained, which at least provided owners with a source of replacement parts.

The Isetta Lives On

Iso, having sold the rights to build its bubblecar in Argentina, also licensed production in France, where it was marketed as the Velam. In concept, this was quite different to the original Iso design, being of monocoque construction with a bolt-on subframe accommodating the engine and drive-train; it also featured a restyled bodyshell. In similar fashion to its Italian and German relations, the Velam was built as a four-wheeler, the wheels having three securing studs instead of four. Being more rounded than other versions, the Velam offered more in the way of interior accommodation, although it remained a two-seater.

Sales of the Velam were compromised from the very beginning because of the niche market that both the Citroën 2CV and Renault 4CV enjoyed. Even when some serious restyling was attempted with the introduction of the Ecrin, customers failed to be motivated, and by 1959 Velam production had ceased.

Brighton – The Home of British Isettas

Dunsfold Tools Ltd was a name that was more or less unknown in the motoring world until it became associated with building Isetta bubblecars under the auspices of Isetta of Great Britain Ltd. The establishment of the British arm of Isetta was

This nicely restored Trojan was pictured at Hebden Bridge in Yorkshire in 1999. Trojan continued building Heinkels until 1965, by which time sales were depressed and orders had reduced to a mere trickle. (H. John Black)

Bubblecars have been put to some pretty unusual uses. This Isetta is fitted with flanged wheels for working at a Welsh slate mine. (Gordon Fitzgerald)

Another aspect of the production process in the BMW factory. (BMW)

One could guess what Stirling Moss is saying to the person looking into this Isetta through the open roof. The banner in the background reads 'The British Manufactured BMW Isetta – World's cheapest car to buy and run'. The car is a Brighton-built vehicle, but the grilles on the door are a feature of American-market cars. (BMW)

formed in 1957 under the shadow of the Suez crisis and petrol rationing. The factory where the Isetta was built was once a locomotive works building steam engines for the London, Brighton and South Coast Railway. The foregoing may not sound out of the ordinary, but it led to the establishment of what was probably the only car factory in the world without any road access. Pedestrian access to the works was via some one hundred steps, and the sole means of transport into, and out of, the works was by rail.

Building Isettas in Britain meant that BMW had a means of access to those markets, such as Canada and Australia, which, together with the United Kingdom, afforded potential sales that would otherwise have eluded the company. There was the added attraction of avoiding expensive tax penalties and adverse currency

rates, to which BMW would have been subjected had the company accessed these markets from Germany. For British trade, this was considered a useful exercise in earning a large return in dollars for a relatively small outlay of deutschmarks, and therefore won the approval of the government. The driving force behind the British end of the enterprise was Captain Ronnie Ashley, the former head of Armstrong-Siddeley's car division.

The enterprise in building Isettas in Britain began in mid-1956 when Dunsfold Tools took over the redundant Brighton locomotive works. When the last steam engine had left the works in March 1957, work started immediately in transforming the engine shed into a car factory, and within three weeks the heavy engineering equipment had been supplanted by jigs and welding

This left-hand-drive Isetta shows the charm of the bubblecar to good effect. With the building of right-hand-drive models the driver sat on the same side of the vehicle as the engine, and a counterweight had to be fitted to the opposite side of the car. (H. John Black)

gear. Production of Isettas then began, and by the third week in April the first cars were coming off the assembly line, having been built by the same people who had previously been responsible for repairing and building railway engines.

Originally, there had been three railway tracks within the locomotive shed, but with the transformation the outer ones had been removed, leaving the centre track for deliveries of components and the export of finished cars. Conveyors were installed in place of the removed tracks as part of the car assembly process.

The presses and jigs for Isetta production were shipped over to Brighton from Bavaria, and even the paint shop was built to BMW's high standards. Engines, transmissions and body panels were imported from Germany, while tyres were supplied by Dunlop (4.80×10in compared to 4.40×10in for German built-vehicles), braking

This American-specification Isetta was pictured in California. Note the door vents and the convertible body style. (Gordon Fitzgerald)

systems by Girling and chassis units by Rubery Owen. Electrical gear, suspension units and accessories were brought in from other component manufacturers in the Midlands or sourced locally.

A few Brighton Isettas were fitted with the Smiths Selectroshift transmission, which did away with the clutch pedal. Far removed from a truly automatic gear change, the Smiths system presented a semi-automatic arrangement whereby pressure placed on the gear selector engaged the clutch electrically. Adding an additional £25 to the cost of an Isetta, demand for the Selectroshift was very small.

Sufficient materials for producing up to 250 Isettas a week were delivered to the workshops by train once a week on a Saturday, and every night sixteen wagons accommodating three cars apiece left the factory for a freight distribution depot in London, and thereafter to specific destinations throughout the country. Build capacity of the Brighton works was 500 vehicles per week, in contrast to BMW's factory which could deliver 220 cars a day.

Both left- and right-hand-drive vehicles could be built at Brighton, and the first 1,000 cars to leave the factory were destined for Canada. These cars differed slightly from those intended for British customers – together with left-hand steering, they were equipped with heavy-duty bumpers and electrical systems that were designed to meet the demanding conditions of North American winters. Isettas were also exported to the USA, these cars being supplied not from Brighton but from BMW's factory in Germany.

In addition to the usual four-wheel models, a three-wheeled Isetta was designed primarily for the British market, where tax arrangements favoured motorized tricycles. Three-wheeler Isettas (referred to as the 'Plus' models) were initially built with left-hand drive and made their introduction in the autumn of 1958. The reason for not adopting right-hand drive was to avoid an imbalance in weight distribution when the driver was the car's sole occupant, and it was not until 1960 that right-hand-drive three-wheelers became available. Performance of three-wheelers was slightly more spirited than their four-wheeled counterparts with in excess of 50mph (80km/h) being easily attainable, even if there was some loss in straight-running stability. Under extreme cornering it was possible to lift one of the front wheels slightly, although only when attempting left turns, something that was absent with the slightly heavier four-wheelers. It has already been mentioned that tyre sizes on Brighton cars differed to those built in Germany; additionally, the rear tyre was oversized (5.20×10in) in the interests of weight distribution and stability.

The conversion to right-hand drive proved to be the cause of some problems at Brighton, not least that having the driver and drive train on the same side of the vehicle produced a tendency for the car to topple over when taking right-hand corners at speed. This was resolved by the fitting of a counterweight to the left-hand side of the car, which was concealed by some deftly placed interior trim. However, it was not unknown for some unsuspecting owner to do away with the counterbalance in ignorance, with dire results!

Isettas exported to Canada were met with somewhat disappointing demand, and those cars that were unsold were returned to England. On arrival back at Brighton they were converted to local specification, although they retained their left-hand steering.

The image of Isetta that accounted for a total production well in excess of 200,000 bubblecars. (BMW)

A Bigger Bubble

In the autumn of 1957 BMW announced a larger version of its Isetta bubblecar, the two-door 600. This was a full four-seat, conventional four-wheeler. Designed to compete with an increasing number of small cars emanating from manufacturers around the world, the BMW 600 was a clever arrangement that used some of the most unique features of the Isetta bubblecar.

Retaining the Isetta's single front-opening door, the 600 also featured a side door, on the opposite side of the car to the driver. In common with its smaller stablemate, the 600 had a steering column with swivel joints, in this instance being double-jointed to allow it to hinge in accordance with the door opening and closing.

The 600's 585cc air-cooled flat twin engine was derived from the well-known BMW R60 motorcycle unit and detuned. Mounted at the rear of the car and positioned behind the divided rear axle, the engine delivered maximum power of 19.5bhp at 4,000rpm to give a top speed of 63mph (101km/h) and fuel consumption of between 45–55mpg (6.3–5.2ltr/100km).

Contemporary media reports suggested that the BMW had similarities to Fiat's 600, the car that, in 1955, succeeded the Topolino. Viewed from the rear there was some affinity between the two cars, but that is where any comparison stopped. The BMW was, in effect, an extended bubble, and its family resemblance with the smaller car was obvious. It was also smaller than the Fiat 600, the wheelbase being 279mm (11in) shorter than that of the Italian car.

The interior of the 600 was more conventional than the bubble's; notwithstanding the single front door, the gearchange and parking brake were centrally positioned, and in the rear compartment the folding seat really did accommodate two adults in reasonable comfort. Access to the car's interior through the front door was similar to the Isetta, but the vehicle's longer body did prevent it from being parked at right angles to the kerb. Street parking had to be carefully planned, as if any car was parked too close to the front of the 600, opening of the front door could be problematic. The spare wheel was carried on

BMW introduced a four-wheel, four-seat 'super-bubble' in the autumn of 1957. Having two doors, one at the front, another at the side, the Isetta 600 proved popular. (BMW)

BMW's claim was that the 600 with its two-cylinder, 585cc air-cooled engine could accommodate four adults and a child, achieve a top speed in excess of 60mph (100km/h) and return 63mpg (4.5ltr/100km). Those owners who succumbed to the 600's charms were not disappointed. (BMW)

This cut-away drawing shows the construction and drive train of the 600. The doors gave easy access to an interior that was both roomy and comfortable.

the inside of the front door, which arguably afforded increased protection in the event of a front-end impact. With the front door closed, the interior of the 600 took on an appearance more associated with a conventional car – the instrument binnacle and spartan facia would not have looked out of place on any number of small European vehicles. For the rear passenger sitting behind the driver there was no exit except through the door on the opposite side of the car.

The chassis of the 600 was a simple box section affair that was nevertheless strong. It had side members that swept upwards at the rear to accommodate the universally jointed drive shafts. In fact, the suspension arrangement with its transverse trailing arms served BMW well over a number of years. It was later used for the 700 model, a true small sporting machine.

The one major problem with the 600 was that it failed to attract customers in the numbers that BMW had anticipated. Neither a true bubblecar, nor having the character of a conventional small car, fewer than 35,000 600s were built in its two-year production span.

5 Messerschmitt

Mention bubblecars and the Messerschmitt will undoubtedly come to mind. Few cars since World War II have been so instantly recognizable, and it is for this reason that the Messerschmitt has claimed for itself a particular charisma. Messerschmitts will always be associated with aeroplanes, for the very good reason that Professor Willy Messerschmitt is recognized as one of Germany's leading aircraft designers.

Tiny and fragile-looking, bug-eyed and definitely claustrophobic; these are just a few of the perceptions that would appear to give the thumbs-down to one of the world's oddest motor vehicles. Yet, for all the seemingly adverse points relating to this motorized tandem, reading through countless road tests and newspaper reports, what could easily have been viewed as one of motoring's spectacular failures in fact emerged as one of its greatest prizes.

In similar fashion to the Heinkel bubblecar, the Messerschmitt, too, came about when an aeroplane designer and builder decided to diversify into motor manufacturing. It has to be said, though, that the end product was more akin to a motor scooter than motor car.

The Messerschmitt is further linked with Heinkel, and for that matter Isetta, in that it made its debut before the Suez crisis. Like its bubblecar cousins, Messerschmitts materialized out of post-war austerity to fulfil a role as essential transport at a time when 'proper' cars were virtually unobtainable in Germany. However, contrary to popular belief that Willy Messerschmitt created the Cabin Scooter concept, it was actually designed by Fritz Fend, a young designer who, during the war, had worked with Professor Messerschmitt. Following hostilities, Fend reasoned that simply engineered forms of personal transport were a necessity. What is important about the events at the time is that Fend's ideas of developing basic forms of motorized transport met with severe difficulties due to the unavailability of raw materials, thus demolishing all those false stories about Messerschmitts being built out of redundant aircraft parts.

The Origins of the Messerschmitt

Unveiled in 1953 at the Geneva Motor Show, the 174cc Messerschmitt Kabinenroller created something of a sensation, not only because of its diminutive size and unique looks, but also because of its gestation from an invalid-carriage design. The fact that the Messerschmitt evolved from such humble beginnings rather than being designed out of aircraft principles makes the history of the Kabinenroller all the more interesting.

Fritz Fend has already been mentioned in an earlier chapter, and it was his design for invalid carriages, an essential form of transportation for the many thousands of soldiers returning from war who had suffered the loss of limbs, that gave him the impetus to design his cabin scooter. Fend unveiled his Flitzer in 1948, complete with fragile body and bicycle wheels. Literally translated as 'to dash', the Flitzer used a treadle as a means of propulsion rather than adopting a cyclic action, which, depending on the user's handicap, did not always prove to be entirely satisfactory. Fend perceived that with the help of a suitably economic motor, transportation could be effectively automated and speeded up. He therefore proposed using a 38cc Victoria single-cylinder engine,

MEJOR CON MESSERSCHMITT

Despite its name, the Messerschmitt had little association with aero technology, other than the fact that the designer and eventual builder were both involved in the aviation industry. The appearance of the microcar, especially with its streamlined shape and plexiglass cabin dome, nevertheless convinced many otherwise.

Fritz Fend

Born in 1919, Fritz Fend had trained as an engineer and during World War II was drafted into working for Messerschmitt, where he helped to design aircraft undercarriages. Following the end of hostilities, he returned to the family home at Rosenheim in Upper Bavaria to help run his father's shop.

However, Fend soon realized that it was engineering that interested him most, and his attention was drawn to the plight of the many injured war veterans who were without any form of transportation. It has been claimed that he was particularly influenced by one ex-soldier who, having had both legs amputated, was reduced to propelling himself around by hand on what was essentially a large skateboard. Deciding that a more dignified and sophisticated means of transport should be made available, Fend set about designing a manually propelled three-wheeled invalid carriage that was, for obvious reasons, constructed out of the most lightweight of materials. It was when he decided that his tricycle should have a tiny motor to aid propulsion that the idea of a minicar for general use in transport-starved Germany materialized. Thus emerged a machine that was designed by Fend, but was built by Messerschmitt and carried the aircraft manufacturer's name. Fritz Fend furthered his interests in economical transportation by establishing a research bureau, which, over a period of several years, produced some highly interesting projects.

which would afford 19mph (30km/h) at best, and return between 230–240mpg (1.2–1.17ltr/100km). Similar engines were mostly attached to bicycles as a means of removing some of the effort of pedalling, and were extensively used throughout Germany and Britain.

Fend had acquired a dilapidated wooden building near to the family business in Rosenheim in which to build his Flitzer. Lathes, machinery and welding equipment were sought at the cheapest possible prices, and often on the black market in exchange for other goods. Because of the political situation in Germany it was necessary to conceal the exact nature of his business, and Fend merely allowed his workshop to be known as Fritz M Fend, Technical Development Works.

Financial help towards producing a viable version of the Flitzer became available when Fend received the backing of the Verband Deutscher Kriegsversehrter (VDK), the Association of War Wounded. This meant that the VDK acknowledged Fend's design as being an aid to those suffering from war injuries and, as a result, provided him with access to supplies of raw materials. The grant from the VDK allowed Fend to use thin sheet metal and a proper, if still elementary, steering control. Fifty single-seat Flitzers were ordered by the VDK, which provided DM10,000 in aid, and further tooling and equipment were forthcoming when the German Ministry of Labour agreed to back Fend financially.

It was in 1949 that a more powerful version of the Flitzer, with a 98cc Fichtel & Sachs engine, went into production. Progression towards such dizzy power had been largely by accident, inasmuch as a newspaper feature had erroneously mentioned the vehicle as having a 350cc engine instead of 38cc. Fend was besieged with orders from hopeful customers which he was unable to fulfil, but at least the affair did provide him with some much-needed publicity and provided the impetus to uprate the power to 98cc. In so doing, the entire concept of the Flitzer changed; instead of bicycle wheels Fend used much smaller wheels, similar to those fitted to wheelbarrows, along with more durable pneumatic tyres.

There was no shortage of customers for the diminutive Flitzer, and the Fichtel & Sachs engine with its two-speed gearbox offered a top speed of nearly 40mph (65km/h). Fichtel & Sachs was impressed by the Flitzer's performance, and although Fend also chose to fit the 98cc Riedel engine as an option so as to provide three speeds, the manufacturers were keen to maintain a good working relationship with the company. The association between Fend and Fichtel & Sachs was to last throughout Messerschmitt production.

The design of the Flitzer evolved into something more substantial between 1949 and 1950, and what emerged from the Rosenheim works was a three-wheeled scooter with the engine

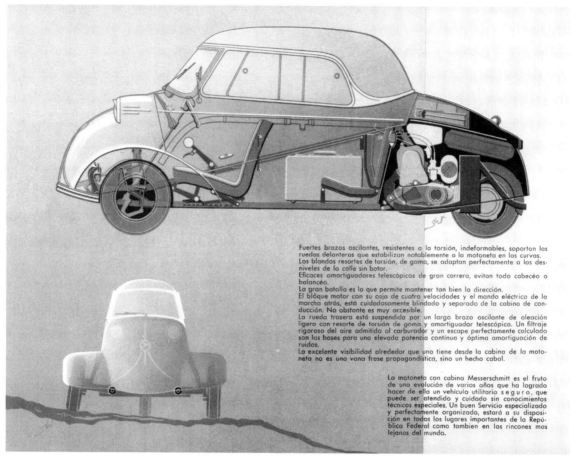

Fuertes brazos oscilantes, resistentes a la torsión, indeformables, soportan las ruedas delanteras que estabilizan notablemente a la motoneta en las curvas.
Los blandos resortes de torsión, de goma, se adaptan perfectamente a los desniveles de la calle sin botar.
Eficaces amortiguadores telescópicos de gran carrera, evitan todo cabecéo o balancéo.
La gran batalla es la que permite mantener tan bien la dirección.
El blóque motor con su caja de cuatro velocidades y el mando eléctrico de la marcha atrás, está cuidadosamente blindado y separado de la cabina de conducción. No obstante es muy accesible.
La rueda trasera está suspendida por un largo brazo oscilante de aleación ligera con resorte de torsión de goma y amortiguador telescópico. Un filtraje rigoroso del aire admitido al carburador y un escape perfectamente calculado son las bases para una elevada potencia continua y óptima amortiguación de ruidos.
La excelente visibilidad alrededor que uno tiene desde la cabina de la motoneta no es una vana frase propagandística, sino un hecho cabal.

La motoneta con cabina Messerschmitt es el fruto de una evolución de varios años que ha logrado hacer de ella un vehículo utilitario s e g u r o , que puede ser atendido y cuidado sin conocimientos técnicos especiales. Un buen Servicio especializado y perfectamente organizado, estará a su disposición en todos los lugares importantes de la República Federal como tambien en los rincones mas lejanos del mundo.

Taken from a contemporary sales brochure, these evocative drawings explain the fundamental design and technical arrangements of the Messerschmitt.

positioned above the trailing wheel; there was accommodation for two people sitting in tandem within a simple cabin that had a lift-up roof and handlebar controls. Fend's Kabinenroller had finally arrived, and everywhere he went in it the vehicle was the subject of immense curiosity. There exists the story that Fend, having parked his machine in a town, returned to find it surrounded by onlookers, a few of whom had manhandled the Kabinenroller in order to examine its underside. By this time, around ten machines a week were leaving Rosenheim, which was about its full capacity, and to produce greater numbers of vehicles meant not only relocating to larger premises but also a sizeable investment in tooling equipment.

Messerschmitt to the Rescue

Unable to finance the expansion of his enterprise alone, Fritz Fend sought financial backing. Fend Kraftfahrzeug GmbH was established towards the end of 1951, but the relationship soon turned sour. Fend's business partners had little or no interest in the product that was being manufactured, being merely interested in absorbing the profits, and within months Fend faced bankruptcy. There was only one solution – Fend bought out his partners, which left him little capital with which to continue trading.

Under the auspices of Fend Kraftfahrzeug GmbH, some 154 Kabinenrollers were produced, most of which were fitted with the 98cc 4.5bhp Riedel engine. Performance was quite impressive, with a maximum speed of nearly 50mph (80km/h), although at this speed fuel consumption, at around 100mpg (2.8ltr/ 100km), was seriously compromised. Not surprisingly, the little Kabinenroller had made for itself a distinct reputation.

Fend's lack of finances led him to consider approaching his old employer, Professor Willy Messerschmitt, whom, he had heard, was looking to take on work while the ban on German armaments remained in force. The Messerschmitt works had diversified into various activities ranging from repairing railway rolling stock to manufacturing sewing machines and building prefabricated homes. The main Messerschmitt factory at Augsburg had been almost totally destroyed by bombing during the war, and thousands of skilled workers including engineers were without work. At his other factory at Regensburg, Messerschmitt had planned to build Vespa scooters under licence, and had further intended to produce medium-size motor cars that were to have been powered by Messerschmitt's own five-cylinder radial engine. The latter proposal did not proceed beyond the prototype stage. Professor Messerschmitt was very much aware of Fritz Fend's Kabinenroller, and he was only too pleased to collaborate with his former employee and engineer. Messerschmitt perceived that such a vehicle, possibly somewhat refined, would be an attractive proposition as an essential but minimal means of transport. One condition that the Professor did make was that the vehicle should carry the Messerschmitt name, as this would add to the car's marketing potential.

The refinements proposed by Messerschmitt amounted to the building of a larger machine than Fend had originally planned. It was essential that there should be accommodation for two people, and the cabin scooter layout was retained in the interest of keeping the drag factor of the

Professor Willy Messerschmitt 1898–1978

Born in Frankfurt, Willy Messerschmitt began experimenting with aeroplanes at the age of twelve, and three years later formed an association with a professional architect to build full-size gliders. At the onset of war in 1914, Messerschmitt was exempted from military service on health grounds and instead pursued technical qualifications at Munich's Institute of Technology.

In 1923 Messerschmitt established his own company building monoplane gliders; the following year the company relocated to a disused brewery at Bamberg where more advanced gliders were constructed ahead of a powered aircraft which took to the air later that year. Always innovative in his designs, Messerschmitt built up a solid reputation, and in 1934 unveiled the Bf 108, which was an unconventional low-wing single-engined four-seater and was the forerunner of the Bf 109 fighter, the mainstay of the Luftwaffe during World War II. During the war Messerschmitt was responsible for a number of notable aircraft, in particular the rocket-powered Me 163 and jet Me 262.

After World War II, Messerschmitt went to Argentina where he established that country's aviation industry; he returned to Germany in the early 1950s. It was always Willy Messerschmitt's intention to resume aircraft building once the ban on Germany's armaments had been lifted, but in the meantime he entered automobile production, building Fritz Fend's cabin scooter, the Kabinenroller, to much acclaim. As a person, Willy Messerschmitt was of reserved nature, often perceived as being preoccupied but nevertheless dignified, and more relaxed at his drawing board than when attending meetings, many of which he considered as being time-wasting and unnecessary. It is known that Messerschmitt never got on with his archrival Ernst Heinkel.

frontal aspect as low as possible in typical aircraft design fashion. Both Fend and Messerschmitt appreciated that the two passengers would sit in tandem, and Fend considered this to be ideal when appealing to motorcyclists and scooterists who were used to having a passenger as pillion. In fact, rear passengers sat with their feet alongside the driver's seat. Rather than having a steering wheel, Fend was adamant that handlebars be used, along with the twist grip controls normally found on a motorcycle. Other design features included minimal suspension, in this instance afforded by rubber bushes, augmented by a large saddle-type spring under the front seat for driver comfort. The rear passenger was devoid of such comfort.

With its low drag factor, Fend's styling of the car's bodywork was deftly streamlined and incorporated many aero-design principles. Stability was aided by the relatively wide front track and the aerodynamic front wings. The high-mounted headlamps were positioned either side of the bridge of the vehicle's nose to give the machine a peculiar bug-eyed appearance, and the side-hinged plexiglass dome of the cabin was reminiscent of an aircraft's cockpit cover. A happy compromise between a motor scooter and a minicar, Fend chose a steel tubular frame combined with a monocoque tub, panelled in sheet steel. The proven Fichtel & Sachs single-cylinder, two-stroke 150cc engine was specified as the power source.

The Messerschmitt makes its Debut

When it was unveiled at the Geneva Motor Show in 1953 the Messerschmitt was at once the centre of close attention. The vehicle on show there was markedly different to that originally proposed by virtue of having a larger engine, a 174cc Fichtel & Sachs in place of the 150cc unit seen on a prototype model. When looking at contemporary press reports of the Geneva show it is easy to accept that the Kabinenroller had been both designed and built by Messerschmitt, and this alone has helped to give an erroneous aspect of the Messerschmitt's history.

Pictured within London's Design Museum, the Messerschmitt makes an interesting comparison with the Ford Cortina. Close examination shows the vehicle to be badged as an FMR.

Testing of the Kabinenroller had been conducted on the formidable Grossglockner Pass in Austria. Whilst the vehicle performed admirably under notoriously difficult conditions, the fitting of the larger engine provided a small but nevertheless essential increase in power. Despite its small size and having only three wheels, the Kabinenroller with its effective power to weight ratio had been able to encounter snow and ice with considerable ease.

The introduction of the Kabinenroller was greeted with some curiosity by those motoring journalists who were unsure whether the vehicle was more scooter than motor car, or whether in fact it was a road-going aeroplane minus its wings. In the event, there was both praise and derision for the Messerschmitt – praise in that the vehicle really did address economical motoring in times of dire austerity, and derision that the car's occupants were encased beneath a plexiglass dome that was reminiscent of Messerschmitt's wartime aeroplanes. Hinged along one side, the cover with its safety-glass screen and two sliding windows opened wide to allow entry and exit of the cabin, and once inside passengers were unkindly referred to as being 'people in aspic'.

A somewhat bizarre feature of the Messerschmitt was that the cockpit cover was hinged along the right-hand side of the car, which meant that when driven in those countries having left-hand drive (including its native Germany), passengers were obliged to enter and alight the vehicle from the road rather than the pavement. Climbing into the confines of the cockpit might have been difficult had it not been for the fact that the front seat moved upwards and rearwards, returning to the normal driving position once the driver was safely ensconced within the cabin. Interior accommodation being at a premium, additional luggage could be carried on a rack pannier-style on the right-hand side of the vehicle, but what this did to the car's performance and handling characteristics can only be imagined. There was sufficient space for a couple of small pieces of baggage in a compartment above the engine, and additionally the rear seat could be easily removed to provide increased carrying capacity.

Messerschmitt KR175

Chassis

Type	Triangulated tubular frame with steel body panels forming stressed skin

Engine

Layout	Fichtel & Sachs fan-cooled single-cylinder two-stroke
Peak power	9.5bhp @ 5,260rpm
Bore×stroke	62×58mm
Cubic capacity	174cc
Compression ratio	6.6:1

Fuel supply

Carburettor	Bing needle-type carburettor with air filter

Electrical

Generator and starter	12V Siba combined starter and dynamo

Transmission

Clutch	Cork-lined clutch, foot-operated
Gearbox	Four-speed gearbox in unit with engine
Drive	Final drive by partially enclosed chain

Brakes

Type	Independent and foot-operated on all three wheels

Suspension

All	All wheels sprung by cylindrical rubber bonded units
Front	Transverse pivoted arms carry front wheels
Rear	Rear wheel mounted on arm formed by chaincase and pivoted about gearbox sprocket centre

Capacity

Fuel tank	11ltr (2.4gal)

Dimensions

Length	2,819mm (9ft 3in)
Width	1,219mm (4ft 0in)
Wheelbase	2,032mm (6ft 8in)
Track	921mm (3ft ¼in)
Weight	406lb (184kg)

Performance (road-test conditions)

Top speed	50mph (80km/h); cruising speed 30–45mph (50km/h–72km/h)
Fuel consumption	123mpg (2.3ltr/100km); average 85mpg (3.4ltr/100km)

Despite any misgivings about the Kabinenroller's diminutive size and alien appearance, orders came rushing into Messerschmitt's sales office. The price of the car had obviously much to do with this – at DM2,100, which pitched it between a substantial motorcycle and the Volkswagen Beetle and others of the least expensive family cars, it was perceived as being extremely good value. Messerschmitt's intention had been to introduce the Kabinenroller at an artificially low price before gradually increasing this to DM2,700. However, as the price rose so sales began to level off, and on reaching DM2,470, the number of orders received went into decline.

Messerschmitt had avoided actually marketing the Kabinenroller as a car, but the British concessionaires, Beulah Hill Engineering Co Ltd of London SE19, enthusiastically referred to the vehicle's car-like attributes – 'London to

Bournemouth on less than a gallon – in saloon-car comfort too!' was the message that appeared in motoring journals. Messerschmitt's advertising was particularly emotive and is viewed today as being a delightful period piece of marketing. Not only was there the obligatory scene of fun-loving innocence, the Kabinenroller completed the picture, with the sea and coastline in the background serving as an evocative backdrop.

By August 1954 Messerschmitt production had reached 200 vehicles weekly, and *Motor Cycling* magazine made the point that such machines as the Kabinenroller were more acceptable within mainland Europe than in Britain, which retained some conservative ideals regarding motor transport. Motorcyclists no doubt appreciated the vehicle's handling characteristics more than car drivers, the direct steering by handlebars being a familiar technique. The handlebar-operated

The same car in the Design Museum, seen in comparison with the Trabant, the people's car that remains a familiar sight on roads throughout Eastern Europe.

Victor Saville's Messerschmitt as pictured some years ago. The tiny proportions of the vehicle are clearly evident, as is the cabin that allowed two people to sit in tandem. (Gordon Fitzgerald)

twist-grip throttle would also have been familiar, although both pedal-operated clutch and brakes would have found favour among car drivers. The car's low centre of gravity and basic suspension would also have been familiar to motorcyclists; cornering, however, could be safely undertaken at speeds that might have been unadvisable for a sidecar outfit. The Messerschmitt's hard suspension came in for some criticism, and while the coil spring under the driver's seat absorbed much of the bumping, the rear passenger suffered some discomfort.

Testing the Messerschmitt, the late John Bolster was emphatic in his praise for the Fichtel & Sachs engine, proclaiming it be the best two-stroke that he had come across. Not quite so efficient was the manually operated windscreen wiper, the handlebar-operated trigger mechanism being awkward to use. Messerschmitt was quick to appreciate the difficulties of such an arrangement and introduced an electrically driven wiper. A range of optional extras made the

Kabinenroller all the more user-friendly: a sun blind to keep out some of the summer heat; a clock; and a radio.

Messerschmitts were sold in the USA where they must have caused a sensation, especially their size in comparison to the average American sedan. When *Sports Car Illustrated* put the Kabinenroller through its paces, the magazine's tester noted that it felt a little bouncy at 40mph (65km/h), and likened it to a light aircraft taxiing across a grass airfield. The Messerschmitt enjoyed a certain appeal with American families, but nevertheless could not be envisaged as anything other than a second car.

The KR175 was produced until 1955, by which time 19,668 examples had been built. Messerschmitts had not only acquired a loyal following, they had also proved themselves in terms of build quality, reliability and economy. When a more powerful version was announced, it was heralded with much enthusiasm by 'Schmitt' owners around the world.

More Power

When the KR200 was introduced in February 1955 some of the many improvements over the earlier Messerschmitt were clearly obvious. The cockpit dome featured a wraparound screen in place of the flat affair; the track was increased and accordingly the wings accommodated cut-away wheel arches. Inside the cabin there was provision for a child's seat alongside the rear passenger, and when not in use this could be transformed into luggage space. A map pocket was fitted to the right of the driving position, and the driving seat also had a map pocket within the backrest. Improved trimming of the cabin made for living with the 'Schmitt all the more comfortable, and of particular note was the handlebar arrangement, which, being made of moulded plastic, was less like that of a motorcycle's and consequently not as austere.

Out of sight, but nonetheless as important as the aforementioned modifications, were revisions to the Messerschmitt's technical specifications. Fritz Fend had been working on designs for a revised Kabinenroller for some time, and his offerings were well received. Modified wings with cut-away wheel arches concealed all-new rubber-in-torsion front suspension, incorporating telescopic dampers to give a much improved ride. A feature, too, was an improved turning circle. In the tail was installed a new and more powerful Fichtel & Sachs engine, a two-stroke, single cylinder of 191cc.

An Export model of the KR200 was also available that had a more lavish specification than the standard model. These models, which in Britain were known as the De Luxe, were instantly recognizable because of their optional two-tone colour scheme. Secondary colours were applied to wing edges and along the bottom of the vehicle beneath an aluminium moulding, although eventually they were limited to the wing peripheries. A number of optional extras were available, and some, such as the windscreen washer were, in effect, more of a necessity because during damp weather the entire vehicle could be doused by road dirt thrown up by vehicles in front.

Messerschmitt KR200	
Chassis	
Type	Welded tubular steel construction
Engine	
Layout	Fichtel & Sachs air-cooled single-cylinder two-stroke
Peak power	12bhp @ 5,250rpm
Bore × stroke	65 × 58mm
Cubic capacity	191cc
Compression ratio	6.3:1
Electrical	
Battery	12V
Generator and starter	135W Siba Dynastart starter-generator; coil ignition
Transmission	
Gearbox	Four-speed gearbox integral with engine
Drive	Final drive by enclosed chain
Brakes	
Type	Cable operated 114mm ($4\frac{1}{2}$in) diameter, foot and hand controlled on all three wheels
Suspension	
Front	Front wheels on stub axles pivoting on rubber bushes, spring units controlled by hydraulic dampers
Rear	Rubber suspension
Steering	
Type	Direct steering without steering box, handlebar controlled; front wheels steered via rubber-mounted divided track rods
Tyres	
Type	8 × 4in
Capacity	
Fuel tank	13.6ltr (3gal)
Dimensions	
Length	2,845mm (9ft 4in)
Width	1,219mm (4ft 0in)
Wheelbase	2,032mm (6ft 8in)
Track	1,067mm (3ft 6in)
Weight	463lb (210kg)
Performance	
Top speed	56mph (90km/h)
Fuel consumption	90mpg (3.14ltr/100km)

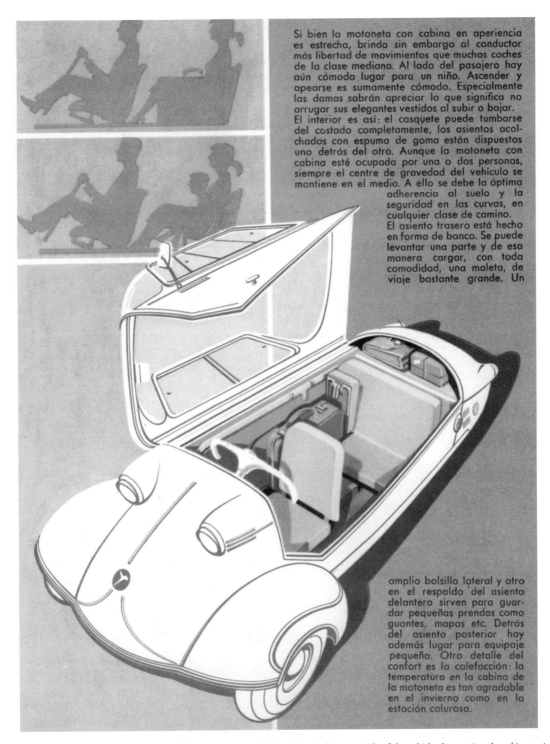

Si bien la motoneta con cabina en apariencia es estrecha, brinda sin embargo al conductor más libertad de movimientos que muchos coches de la clase mediana. Al lado del pasajero hay aún cómoda lugar para un niño. Ascender y apearse es sumamente cómodo. Especialmente las damas sabrán apreciar lo que significa no arrugar sus elegantes vestidos al subir o bajar.

El interior es así: el casquete puede tumbarse del costado completamente, los asientos acolchados con espuma de goma están dispuestos uno detrás del otro. Aunque la motoneta con cabina esté ocupada por una o dos personas, siempre el centre de gravedad del vehículo se mantiene en el medio. A ello se debe la óptima adherencia al suelo y la seguridad en las curvas, en cualquier clase de camino.

El asiento trasero está hecho en forma de banco. Se puede levantar una parte y de esa manera cargar, con toda comodidad, una maleta, de viaje bastante grande. Un amplio bolsillo lateral y otro en el respaldo del asiento delantero sirven para guardar pequeñas prendas como guantes, mapas etc. Detrás del asiento posterior hay además lugar para equipaje pequeño. Otro detalle del confort es la calefacción: la temperatura en la cabina de la motoneta es tan agradable en el invierno como en la estación calurosa.

The cabin opening arrangement is clearly evident, the entire unit being hinged along one side of the vehicle. In practice, the cabin top is heavy, and care has to be taken getting in and out of the car in relation to passing traffic.

An addition to the Messerschmitt range was the Cabriolet version in 1956, the KR201. Attractively finished in De Luxe trim, the KR201 featured black interior upholstery picked out in imitation snakeskin. New rear-view mirrors and chromium-plated rear lights added to the specification, while the hood was finished in black material with silver piping. For those owners who felt uncomfortable locked beneath the heavy transparent dome, the Cabrio was a suitable alternative. A particular feature of the Cabrio was that the hood and plexiglass dome from the Cabin Scooter were interchangeable, something which owners of both cars appreciated. The Cabin Scooter's plexiglass dome was vulnerable to damage, especially if left in the open position, and replacing it with a fabric hood was often a practical solution.

Two additional models also made their debut, the Cabrio-Limousine and the Sport. The former model was more akin to the Cabin Scooter, but featured a rollback hood, making it a convertible. The Sport, however, had a rigid body with just a tonneau for protection. Sales of these two derivatives were vastly outnumbered by the Cabin Scooter and Cabrio and they are therefore rarely seen today.

A charming essay in living with a Messerschmitt appeared in *The Autocar*, the author of the piece proclaiming that an average-sized man was able to wear his hat in the car and be able to arrive at his office warm, dry and tidy. By January 1957 it was estimated that around 350 Messerschmitts had been imported to Britain from Germany, but already there were rumours that production might cease. The number of Messerschmitts on

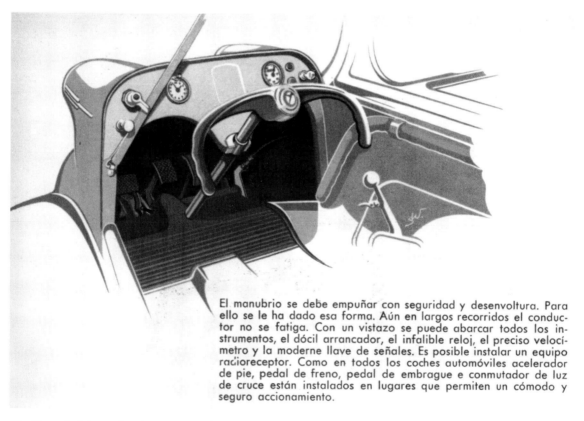

El manubrio se debe empuñar con seguridad y desenvoltura. Para ello se le ha dado esa forma. Aún en largos recorridos el conductor no se fatiga. Con un vistazo se puede abarcar todos los instrumentos, el dócil arrancador, el infalible reloj, el preciso velocímetro y la moderne llave de señales. Es posible instalar un equipo radioreceptor. Como en todos los coches automóviles acelerador de pie, pedal de freno, pedal de embrague e conmutador de luz de cruce están instalados en lugares que permiten un cómodo y seguro accionamiento.

The Messerschmitt's controls and instruments as depicted by a Spanish market sales catalogue. For those owners new to the Messerschmitt, handling characteristics were quite different to that of a conventional car, and more like that of a motor scooter.

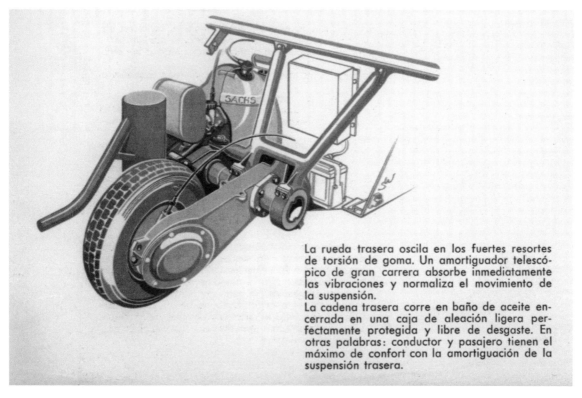

La rueda trasera oscila en los fuertes resortes de torsión de goma. Un amortiguador telescópico de gran carrera absorbe inmediatamente las vibraciones y normaliza el movimiento de la suspensión.
La cadena trasera corre en baño de aceite encerrada en una caja de aleación ligera perfectamente protegida y libre de desgaste. En otras palabras: conductor y pasajero tienen el máximo de confort con la amortiguación de la suspensión trasera.

Early Messerschmitts were powered by a single-cylinder 174cc Fichtel & Sachs two-stroke engine, although the prototype design was fitted with a 150cc unit. The KR175 was replaced by the KR200 in February 1955. The new model was fitted with an all-new 191cc Fichtel & Sachs engine, which is depicted here.

British roads was but a fraction of the output from Regensburg where, at the end of 1956, the figure stood at some 20,840 vehicles.

FMR is Established

In January 1957 Messerschmitt vehicle production transferred from Messerschmitt to Fahrzeug und Maschinebau GmbH (FMR). Professor Willy Messerschmitt, like his old adversary, Ernst Heinkel, had always intended returning to aircraft production, and to do so meant the termination of his vehicle manufacturing interests.

Messerschmitt's car-making activities were, by late 1956, making a loss and that part of the company was put up for sale. Auto-Union and Zündapp were interested parties, and so was Maschinebau Knott Eggstatt, a company that had

produced a number of components for Messerschmitt. Fend foresaw that his future lay with Valentine Knott of MARKE rather than Auto-Union and Zundapp, and formed a partnership to be known as FMR.

The transfer of production to FMR should have been relatively smooth, but was marred to a certain extent by some political issues. Both Fritz Fend and Willy Messerschmitt had agreed to the Augsburg Eagle badge remaining on the nose of the car, along with the Messerschmitt name being carried on the side of the vehicle. External events, however, caused it to be replaced by a new logo, the design of which was three linked circles carrying the company initials. The change to the new badge had been in response to a claim by Mercedes that the profile of the Augsburg Eagle within a circle was too much like its own

In addition to saloons, Messerschmitts were built as convertibles, one such pictured at Arizona in 1979. The model is the KR200; note the American specification bars front and rear.

three-pointed star. No sooner was the affair with Mercedes finalized, but it was the turn of Auto-Union to raise objection to FMR's badge. Auto-Union declared that the linked circles were too much like its own four-linked badge and there-fore a further change, to three linked diamonds, was made.

Super Messerschmitt

During this period in Messerschmitt history Fritz Fend was showing much creativeness; not only had he spent considerable time preparing the KR200 and its derivatives, he was also active in further developing his microcar theme. One par-ticular development was the introduction of a Messerschmitt 'special' that was built for record breaking and endurance testing. Fend chose the KR200 as a basis for his design and, in addition to increasing the power of the vehicle, he clad it with a specially designed wind-cheating body. With its streamlined body the KR200 Super

looked as powerful as it was, but under that svelte exterior there nevertheless existed much of the Kabinenroller's running gear. While the KR200 was attracting much attention and earning impressive reviews in the media, Fend decided that more should be done to promote the Messerschmitt image.

The success of the record-breaking run had obvious advantages regarding sales of new Messerschmitts, and the car's reliability was unquestioned. As for future developments, Fend proposed something all the more exciting.

The Messerschmitt Tiger – Tg500

Of all the Messerschmitts none is so fabled as the Tiger. Distinguishable as being the only four-wheeled Kabinenroller, it was also the largest, and quite definitely the fastest. Based on the design of the KR200, it was powered by a specially developed twin-cylinder, two-stroke engine of 490cc capacity.

Messerschmitt Record-Breaker

The Hockenheim race track in West Germany was the venue for one of the most extraordinary events in post-war automotive history. On the morning of 29 August 1955, a team of engineers rolled a tiny but aerodynamic three-wheeled motor car on to the tarmac in readiness to challenge an endurance record attempt. A team of six drivers was standing by to propel the Messerschmitt throughout a 24-hour marathon drive. The aim was to break through a target speed that meant maintaining an average of 65mph (105km/h).

The team of six comprised drivers Bonsch, Strumm, Eisele, Rathjen, Dr Schwind and Fend. It was evident from the start of the marathon that the 191cc Messerschmitt was capable of successfully completing the challenge, and along the straight sections of track was edging towards 78mph (126km/h). Lap after lap an average speed of 66.5mph (107km/h) was being maintained, and it was only during the final hours of the event that unforeseen problems began to emerge. Foggy conditions brought the average speed down to 59mph (95km/h), and when the weather further deteriorated it was necessary to light straw bales along the edges of the track in order to mark its boundaries.

At the end of the marathon the Messerschmitt team had achieved twenty-one new endurance records, and three existing records held by larger-engined cars had also been smashed.

Although universally known as the Tiger, this Messerschmitt was never officially designated as such. Fritz Fend had originally proposed the name, but he quickly met with opposition as the name was already in use. Ultimately Tg500 was viewed as being a viable alternative, as it not only gave a positive indication as to the engine size, but Tg was sufficiently close to Tiger as a word, especially in the German language.

To Messerschmitt enthusiasts the Tg500 is the ultimate model. Fewer than a thousand examples were built and only fourteen were officially imported into the United Kingdom. Of those fourteen only two are unaccounted for, the remainder all being very closely guarded. As a specific model there were some problems regarding customer appeal – certainly the increased power over that of the KR200 was a strong point but, ultimately, the vehicle remained a two-seater in tandem along with precious little luggage accommodation.

When introduced in 1957 there were criticisms from within the motoring press that a full-width body style to enable passengers to sit side by side had not been adopted. Had it been, no doubt the vehicle's aerodynamics would have been considerably compromised, and furthermore the entire concept of the original design would have been lost.

The most sought-after of all Messerschmitts is the Tg500, which is often, but incorrectly, referred to as the Tiger. Whilst the Tg500 was developed from the KR200, it was built by FMR as a four-wheeler and fitted with a Fichtel & Sachs 494cc two-stroke engine. Close examination reveals larger wheels and wider wings to accommodate the increased performance, and larger diameter brakes were hydraulically operated. (Gordon Fitzgerald)

Messerschmitt seen in the company of a Peel (centre) and Heinkel (right). All three cars were owned by Gordon Fitzgerald when this photograph was taken. (Gordon Fitzgerald)

Immediately noticeable about the Tg500 is its extended tail, which is necessary in order to house the Fichtel & Sachs twin two-stroke. Locked on to the engine cowling was the spare wheel, which was relocated from its earlier position above the engine. If two passengers were also carried, this led to considerable extra weight at the rear of the vehicle, and under some circumstances produced tail-heavy characteristics when the machine was put through its paces. That the car could be thrown round bends without there being any real feel of roll was, nevertheless, to its credit. Following a pretty active period with a Tg500, *The Autocar* tester was moved to remind readers of the importance of raising tyre pressures, 3psi at the front and 5psi at the rear, to afford the best handling qualities when driving at high speeds. A particular feature of the car which was experienced on its introduction was the abnormally high top gear ratio, which only came into its own when on the open road. For town driving, third gear was quite adequate, there being a considerable gap between second and third ratios.

FMR advertising presented the Tg500 as a true sportscar and reminded potential owners that terrific acceleration could propel the car to 65mph (105km/h) in third gear. Safety was, of course, the prime issue, and the low centre of gravity made, so customers were assured, overturning impossible. Mountain gradients presented no problem to the Tiger, and for town driving where there were narrow streets and dense traffic, the slim shape of the vehicle came into its own. Feather-light steering, large diameter hydraulic brakes, independent rear suspension, racing bucket seats, aerodynamic styling and powerful headlights all combined to produce a very special package.

Messerschmitt Tg500

Chassis	
Type	Torsion-proof tubular steel frame with completely enclosed floor

Engine	
Layout	FMR twin-cylinder two-stroke
Peak power	20bhp @ 5,000rpm
Bore×stroke	67×70mm
Cubic capacity	490cc
Compression ratio	6.5:1

Fuel supply	
Carburettor	Three-stage Bing

Electrical	
Starter	Bosch 12V Dynostarter

Transmission	
Clutch	Two-plate dry clutch
Gearbox	Gearbox in engine block, four speeds and reverse
Drive	Final drive to rear wheels via spur wheel and differential to articulate drive shafts

Brakes	
Type	Hydraulic, foot-operated on all four wheels; parking brake on front wheels

Suspension	
Front	Independent suspension with progressive springing; hydraulic shock absorbers; torsion rubber sprung front wheels
Rear	Self-acting stabilising control; coil-sprung rear wheels

Steering	
Type	Direct; modern steering bar with fingertip controls for lighting and trafficators
Turning circle	Left: 9,550mm (31ft 4in); right: 8,788mm (28ft 10in)

Tyres	
Type	4.40×10in

Capacity	
Fuel tank	30ltr ($6\frac{1}{2}$gal)

Dimensions	
Length	3,048mm (10ft 0in)
Width	1,295mm (4ft 3in)
Wheelbase	1,892mm (6ft $2\frac{1}{2}$in)
Track	Front: 1,116mm (3ft 8in); rear: 1,041mm (3ft 5in)
Weight	770lb (350kg)

Performance	
Top speed	approx. 90mph (145km/h)
Fuel consumption	52mpg (5.43ltr/100km)

'As powerful as a Tiger' was FMR's marketing message. The car was introduced into Europe on 5 May 1958, and into Britain some four months later on Monday, 29 September 1958. The venue for the Tiger's debut was Brands Hatch, but unknown to the media the car was actually seen publicly the day before at a Messerschmitt club event at Narborough in the Midlands. Fritz Fend had accepted an invitation on behalf of the Messerschmitt club to provide members with a preview and demonstration of the car.

That the Tiger holds a very special affection for Messerschmitt owners is obvious. On the day of the special preview, 'Schmitters from all around the country converged on Narborough and were given an exhilarating demonstration of the car's abilities by Fend in his personal vehicle.

That the Tiger's handling and cornering characteristics were nothing less than exceptional was conveyed by Fend, who argued that the machine out-performed many sports cars. The rear suspension layout with its self-compensating toe-in arrangement was ahead of its time, and Fend could never understand why this characteristic had not been applied previously.

The Tg500 remained in production at Regensburg until early in 1964. At the same time, production of the KR200 came to an end. The spirit of the Messerschmitt did, however, live on, for a little time at least. One of the final batches of engines was exported to Australia where they were used to power the Lightburn Zeta sports car. Along with the Isetta and Heinkel, the Messerschmitt will long be regarded as having a very special place in motoring history.

6 Small is Beautiful

Post-war austerity meant that the quest for economical motoring remained important until well into the 1950s. The demand for inexpensive cars that had arisen in the late 1940s showed no signs of abating, and when the Suez crisis manifested itself, the need for economy became all the more acute. While some minicars and bubblecars were adept in providing long and reliable service, often with examples producing extraordinary mileages under sometimes unsympathetic conditions, a number of vehicle types appeared to be simply too fragile or diminutive to produce anything like energetic motoring. That said, there have been some remarkable instances where even the smallest and minimally powered machines have survived almost unthinkable feats of endurance. Some of the vehicles under discussion in this chapter would make Isettas, Heinkels and Messerschmitts appear wholly substantial by comparison, and of course the microcar scene would have been all the poorer without them.

While such cars as the Messerschmitt and the other microcars were an obvious choice among those motorists intent on minimal motoring, there was a plethora of other vehicles that successfully served a particular role in attracting customers. If smallness of size was the criteria, then the Peel's absolute minimalism was of obvious advantage. The Peel was a product of the Isle of Man, a location that played a specific role in formative motor racing and which was home to the Tourist Trophy events throughout the early part of the twentieth century.

Smallest of the Bubbles – The Peel

For use on the Isle of Man, the Peel had certain advantages. These minute machines were able to negotiate the island's narrow roads and lanes with the greatest of ease, and the lowly top speed of the car really seemed not to matter. However, they only offered accommodation for one, and this is the clue to the Peel being the smallest car built in the United Kingdom. The fate of the Peel P50 was secured virtually at its introduction, which was late by bubblecar standards. The car made its debut in 1962, three years after the Mini had made its mark on the world, and at a time when the microcar era was, for the time being, on the wane.

When the Peel Engineering Co. launched its fibreglass box-on-wheels this was not the first time it had proposed motor car production. Peel's first foray into the automotive world was in 1955 when it announced a highly interesting little machine known as the Manxcar. Unlike the later P50, the Manxcar offered accommodation for two adults and two children, all within an overall length of 2,286mm (90in); the styling was not unattractive and was unusual in that it used fibreglass at a time when the product was still in its infancy. Peel Engineering specialized in fibreglass mouldings for boats and motorcycle fairings and therefore the idea of building a car using the same material was a logical progression. The Manxcar was designed as a three-wheeler with a trailing rear wheel and powered by a 350cc British Anzani engine. A reduction in engine size meant that the car would have been specified with a 250cc motor of the same type had the car gone into production. A further notable aspect of the Manxcar's design was its two 'safety' doors, which rotated upwards and rearwards about a pivot situated at the lower rear corner so as not to open outwards.

Claimed to be the smallest car built in the United Kingdom, the Peel was the product of Peel Engineering on the Isle of Man. Depicted here is the P50, introduced in 1962, a date somewhat late by bubblecar standards. (Gordon Fitzgerald)

Gordon Fitzgerald demonstrates that Peels are relatively easy to manhandle. The car in question is the same as shown in the previous picture but prior to restoration. Some of Gordon's other microcars can be seen – nearest the camera is a Bond Bug, then a Bond 875, Scootacar, Messerschmitt and Heinkel. (Gordon Fitzgerald)

Had the Manxcar entered production there is every reason to believe that it would have been a success. Designed to sell at a fraction under £300 including purchase tax, it had been intended to sell the car additionally in kit form, which would have avoided customers paying any taxes at all. Only one Manxcar was built, which was used for publicity purposes; it was sold to an Island customer and the car's fate remains unrecorded. Problems in exporting the Manxcar to mainland Britain was the chief reason for the car not being produced.

The Peel Engineering Co. was encouraged to reconsider car production in the wake of the bubblecar boom. The prototype P50 on making its debut was shown to have a single wheel at the front, but it would appear that the wheel layout caused Peel engineers some problems because when the car went into production, the single wheel was at the rear. There was also some restyling, and the production car was substantially larger – by 76mm (3in) in length and 152mm

(6in) in width. Stability was always a problem with the P50, and only truly smooth surfaces could be traversed with any real ease. Surviving archive film of P50s on test on the Isle of Man shows the cars skipping and bouncing rather precariously. Around seventy-five P50s were built, a number of which have survived. The car was the centre of controversy from the outset, mainly because of its size, a mere 1,321mm (52in) in length, its tiny 127mm (5in) wheels and a decidedly cramped interior.

The performance of the Peel was somewhat lethargic. 'Car comfort with moped costs' were the main selling points, and for possibly good reason there was no mention of the vehicle's top speed, which was approximately 35mph (56km/h) at best on ideal surface conditions. The engine was a 49cc DKW affair positioned beneath the driver and propelling the rear wheel via a chain and a three-speed gearbox. There was simply no requirement for reverse gear; the car's light weight and provision of a handle at the back

Peel P50

Chassis		**Suspension**	
Type	Triangular frame and fibreglass body	Type	Fully independent; telescopic coil spring units and nylon bushes
Engine		**Tyres**	
Layout	DKW fan-cooled two-stroke	Type	3.5 × 5in
Peak power	4.2bhp	**Capacity**	
Cubic capacity	49cc	Fuel tank	6.8ltr (1½gal) (25/1 petrol/oil mixture)
Transmission			
Gearbox	Three-speed; no reverse	**Dimensions**	
Drive	Chain final drive	Length	1,321mm (4ft 4in)
Brakes		Width	3ft 3in (990mm)
Type	Cable-operated foot brake on front wheels, hand brake operating on rear	Weight	130lb (59kg)
		Performance	
		Top speed	35mph (56km/h)
		Fuel consumption	95mpg (2.97ltr/100km)

were all that were needed for the driver to push it into position. Selling for under £200, each Peel was individually built and it can be said that no two cars were exactly alike. For this affordable price the car was delivered in a wooden box, which, it was claimed, could be used as a garage!

In 1965 Peel introduced an all-new microcar, the Trident. This was a bubblecar in the full sense, in that the two occupants sat within a largely transparent cocoon. The success or otherwise of the P50 had been the springboard towards developing a larger and arguably more attractive minicar which incorporated some unusual design details. Sharing the P50's 49cc engine and tiny wheels, the decidedly cuddly shaped Trident was nevertheless quite different from its predecessor,

An all-new Peel was introduced in 1965, which was known as the Trident. This really was a bubblecar and two examples are pictured here either side of a P50. (Gordon Fitzgerald)

and its construction was somewhat novel. The vehicle was built as two main components, one comprising a floorpan together with a sub-assembly housing the engine, along with an interior that was moulded in much the same way as would be expected of a small boat. The moulding incorporated the seats, on to which the simple vinyl upholstery was attached, and the material-clad footwells. Behind the seats an aperture in the moulding would hold a limited amount of luggage. The second main component was the upper body comprising the frontal assembly complete with direction indicators and headlamps, as well as the plexiglass dome which incorporated a flat safety-glass windscreen.

Constructed as two essential assemblies, the top section of the Trident hinged forwards to afford access to the base, which was built as a moulded fibreglass unit with a small triangular chassis. The large expanse of the canopy – which in this instance has been damaged – could produce some uncomfortable conditions within the cabin during hot or humid weather. (Gordon Fitzgerald)

Inside the cabin conditions could get extremely claustrophobic in hot or humid weather, and the only ventilation was via a small sliding side hatch that was just about large enough for the driver to put an arm through in order to make hand signals. The complete upper body was front hinged to allow it to be tilted upwards and forwards to afford access. The barest of instruments and controls were fitted, and the steering wheel was a one-piece affair very much in the vogue of the Citroën DS and the 2CV-derived Bijou cars of the 1950s and 1960s.

Peel had plans to export the Trident with a larger 125cc Triumph Tina Scooter engine. One particular export market was Canada, but owing to several problems, not least the car's stability and the supply of parts, the project was eventually abandoned. Production of the Trident finished in 1966, by which time some fifty examples had been sold; almost miraculously, surviving cars continue to be discovered.

In the early 1980s, the Japanese car maker Suzuki produced a microcar on very similar lines to that of the Peel. With two tiny wheels at the front and one trailing, Suzuki's Community Vehicle was almost a Trident lookalike. Updated in concept, it featured an air-conditioned cabin and a 50cc engine that permitted a top speed of 20mph (32km/h). Unlike the Trident, Suzuki's CV was a single-seater.

From Railway Engines to Microcars – The Scootacar

Mention the name Hunslet to any railway locomotive enthusiast and they'll immediately recognize the name. Scootacar, on the other hand, may not be so instantly identifiable to motoring enthusiasts. The Leeds-based Hunslet company, respected for its tough and reliable locos, diversified into motor car production in 1957, although the car's designer, Henry Brown, had previously been involved in developing the Rodley car. The Rodley's claim to fame is that it was (arguably) among the worst cars ever produced in Britain.

The story behind the Scootacar is that Henry

This is one way of transporting a pair of Peels! (Gordon Fitzgerald)

Brown merely took a minimal piece of metal to make a crude chassis, placed a Villiers two-stroke engine ahead of the single rear wheel and built around it a fibreglass body of the meanest dimensions. The fact that the driver of the Scootacar sat immediately above the engine and controlled the vehicle by handlebars is evidence enough that the seemingly unlikely accounts of the Scootacar's birth are quite feasible.

The shape of the Scootacar could not have been less appealing – a bubble certainly, but an upright one with a top-heavy stance. The fibreglass body was made in two portions and joined together so that the seal ran up the front of the car, along the roof and down the back. One door was fitted, sensibly on the nearside for the home market, and there was room enough for two occupants, at a squeeze, sitting in tandem.

Scootacar owners actually found their cars to be relatively stable because most of the weight was at the base of the vehicle. Engine vibration led to some uncomfortable journeys, especially for the driver who sat astride the 197cc unit.

Scootacars found favour with customers who appreciated the vehicle's build quality. In 1960, a Mark 2 model was introduced, which was both larger and more stylish than its predecessor. It could accommodate two adults in relative comfort, and there was sufficient room for at least one child as well as a limited amount of luggage. A larger 250cc engine was specified which was tucked away behind the rear seat, and aesthetically the car was all the better for having a bulbous front and an elongated tail.

In 1961 a Mark 3 Scootacar was launched with a 324cc two-stroke twin engine, which gave the

Despite its upright and top-heavy appearance, the Scootacar had a low centre of gravity. Like the Messerschmitt, Scootacars featured handlebar steering.

Mark 2 and Mark 3 Scootacars were differently styled to the Mark 1. Increased interior accommodation meant that a child could be carried in addition to two adults. The Mark 2 was fitted with a 250cc engine and the Mark 3 with a 324cc two-stroke twin. This is Gordon Fitzgerald's Mark 3 pictured in the company of his son. (Gordon Fitzgerald)

Scootacar

Chassis

Type — Welded box-section frame with sheet steel floor

Engine

Layout — Mark 1: Villiers air-cooled single-cylinder two-stroke (Mark 2: 250cc single-cylinder two-stroke; Mark 3: 324cc twin-cylinder)

Peak power — 8.4bhp @ 4,500rpm
Bore × stroke — 59 × 72mm
Cubic capacity — 197cc
Compression ratio — 7.25:1

Electrical

Battery — 12V; Siba Dynastart; coil ignition

Transmission

Clutch — Four-plate foot-operated
Gearbox — Four-speed gearbox in unit with engine

Brakes

Type — Lockheed hydraulic at front and cable-operated hand brake at rear

Suspension

Front — Independent by varying rate coil springs
Rear — Armstrong unit

Tyres

Type — Michelin 4 × 8in

Capacity

Fuel tank — 12.5ltr (2¾gal)

Dimensions

Length — 2,137mm (7ft 0in)
Width — 1,321mm (4ft 4in)
Wheelbase — 1,372mm (4ft 6in)
Height — 1,511mm (4ft 11½in)
Weight — 500lb (227kg)

Performance

Top speed — 55mph (89km/h)
Fuel consumption — 60mpg (4.7ltr/100km)

car an almost frightening top speed of nearly 70mph (113km/h). Some twenty Mark 3s were sold, but Hunslets persevered with the Mark 2 until 1965, by which time a total of around 1,000 Scootacars had been built.

Henry Brown's earlier foray into the minicar business with the short-lived Rodley gave rise to a tiny four-seater of unremarkable design and styling. A four-wheeler with a JAP twin-cylinder 750cc engine, the Rodley really was the epitome of austerity and utility engineering. Having a steel body with the luxury of a fabric sunroof, the car had rather more grand aspirations than its presence belied. It was built for a few months only and attracted no more than sixty-five customers.

It would seem that no Rodleys have survived the years from when the first example took to the road in 1954. Contemporary reports imply that

those customers who were sufficiently brave to endure the virtues of this Yorkshire-built micro-car experienced a number of mechanical problems, not least that the heat from the exhaust pipe caused at least one vehicle to ignite. Engine vibration appears to have been another difficulty that could have been overcome with time, but the lack of sales and poor publicity were to be the early demise of this little vehicle.

Smaller and Smaller . . .

A number of unlikely microcars made their mark in the mid-1950s against all odds. Among the most unique was the Brütsch Mopetta, a smoothly shaped monocar that more resembled a motorized sidecar and which utilized handlebar steering and motorcycle controls. This tricar with its 49cc Sachs moped engine and single

Notwithstanding the condition of this Mark 1 Scootacar, the model attracted a high reputation for its build quality. Driver and passenger sat in tandem, the driver perched above the 197cc Villiers engine, and there was an unusual amount of space for shopping and luggage, something not universally found with such vehicles. (Gordon Fitzgerald)

The designer of the Scootacar was Henry Brown, who had previously developed the Rodley, a four-wheeled minicar powered by a 750cc twin-cylinder JAP engine. Rodleys made their appearance in 1954 and were not noted for their reliability, at least one example having ignited owing to excess exhaust heat. Note the upright door handle and utilitarian stance of the car.

front wheel had a Cyclops lamp neatly faired into its rounded nose, and the car's trim styling should have led to a wide appeal. However, mass production evaded the Mopetta and only fourteen were built.

Related to the Mopetta was the Brütsch-designed Rollera, which shared much of the former's styling. Equipped with a 125cc engine, this fledgling could reach in excess of 50mph (80km/h), owing to the car's light weight of 123kg (270lb). It has to be said that the design of the Rollera was hardly practical, and there is no indication as to how many of these cars were actually built or sold.

Continuing its utilitarian theme, the Rodley's interior was distinctly spartan.

More akin to a motorized sidecar on wheels was the Brütsch Mopetta, which was designed by Egon Brütsch of stocking manufacture fame. Unbelievably tiny, no more than fourteen Mopettas were built. (Gordon Fitzgerald)

Egon Brütsch

Known for developing racing cars, Egon Brütsch was in fact a stocking manufacturer who had a passion for motor cars. He designed several small cars, among which was the Sparrow, or Spatz, but most, because of his limited finances, never materialized beyond the drawing board or prototype stage. Brütsch is possibly best known for the Mopetta, which, had his ideas evolved as planned, might have gone into mass production courtesy of Georg von Opel, a member of the Opel car-building family but not one with immediate connections to it. Opel's campaign proved to be ill-fated and the Mopetta fell into oblivion.

Another of Brütsch's designs. was the Avolette, which retained the Mopetta's rounded features but was larger and had the third wheel at the rear. Five versions of the Avolette were listed in the sales catalogue, one being a saloon with a bubble canopy and opening roof. Mopettas and other Brütsch-designed cars were sold in the UK, namely through Bruetsch Cars (England) and MPHW Sales who were minicar specialists that regularly advertised in the motoring press.

On much the same principle as the Mopetta was the Tourette, a product of Carr Brothers of Purley, Surrey. Carr's Service Manager, A.J. Merkelt, was given the dubious task of developing the Tourette, and he designed the vehicle around a Villiers 8E engine. Merkelt's aim was to build a tiny car that would not only be inexpensive to build but would offer the very cheapest motoring. It had a rounded open tourer body with very effective streamlining including faired-in headlamps. The three-wheeler with a single trailing wheel was eventually given a canopy over the cockpit, but even this extent of finesse did not allow it to proceed beyond the prototype stage.

The French, having a long tradition of building unconventional minicars, produced the Chantecler in 1956. Designed very much on the same principle as the Mopetta and Tourette, the Chantecler was underpowered and little more than 30mph (50km/h) could be attained from its feeble 125cc engine. Built with a fibreglass body, the car was almost perfectly round in shape, with weather protection supplied by nothing more than a simple canvas roof.

Looking something like a Messerschmitt was an Austrian minicar, the Felber. Known for side-cars, Felber & Co diversified into microcar production in 1953 with a vehicle that had two outboard front wheels and one at the rear. The Autoroller, as it was known, had a simple chassis and a 350cc two-stroke engine with four-speed transmission. Development produced a car of more aesthetic styling; the front wheels were encased within substantial wings, and a small number of machines were clad with specialist coachwork, much in the style of the Mathis that was mentioned in a previous chapter, to make them more streamlined. Remarkably, Felbers were used for racing, which made for a highly entertaining spectacle.

One of the foremost names in the British motor industry, BSA, also became embroiled in microcar development. Seeking to further its range of motorcycles, the company, under the direction of managing director Edward Turner, decided to build a simple but minute two-seater, which, in effect, was no more than a three-wheeled motor scooter. Unofficially designated the Ladybird, the prototype BSA was deftly styled, featuring a one-piece body, two pod-shaped headlamps and narrow wings. Access to the 250cc engine, which was positioned ahead of the rear wheel, was by means of a rear-hinged hatch behind the cabin. Having an open body without even a hood, the driver was open to the elements; there were no doors, and the driver, who steered the Ladybird by means of a handle-bar, simply stepped down into the vehicle. Later development added a rudimentary hood. Equipment, controls and instrumentation were sparse – the Ladybird was without a windscreen wiper or direction indicators, but at least braking was efficient and compensated to afford even pressure at each wheel. Switchgear was borrowed from the BSA Sunbeam motor scooter.

Development work on the little BSA was conducted in almost total secrecy, to the extent that the majority of personnel at the BSA works were quite unaware of the project's existence. Work began on preparing the prototype car during the summer of 1960, and was complete by the autumn. The theory behind the development was to build a British bubblecar that would rival those already enjoying some popularity. The selling price, it was decided, would be £283. The chassis and body were built in-house at BSA courtesy of Carbodies, and the styling of the coachwork was exceptionally delightful but nevertheless very costly and complex to build. By the time the Ladybird was ready to go into production the bubblecar era had effectively come to an end and the scheme was abandoned after a second prototype was built.

7 From Oak Trees to Acorns

When some of the most respected names in the motor industry decided to enter the minicar market, many of those motorists who had previously overlooked the trend towards minimal motoring quickly took notice.

Apart from BMW in Germany, there were few mainstream European car makers who bridged the divide to microcars. Elsewhere, Japan's auto manufacturers have, since the 1950s, successfully introduced tiny cars alongside their other more conventional models.

British companies that ventured into microcars as a diversification from more sporting machines include Allard, AC and Fairthorpe. Both Reliant and Bond started building sports cars having already specialized in the economy market, but an altogether more intriguing alliance concerned the famed Lea Francis marque and the Fuldamobil courtesy of the Nobel, which is discussed in an earlier chapter. When the Englishman Captain Raymond Flowers devised the Phoenix sports car when he was living in Egypt, he also designed a microcar. Flowers left Egypt at the time of the Suez crisis, and on his return to Britain he established a partnership with the respected engine maker Henry Meadows to build his microcar. This evolved as the Frisky, details of which will be found in Chapter 9. As for Bond, that car's creator was also responsible for two other models, the tiny Berkeley sports car, and the Unicar that was built by tractor manufacturer Opperman.

The Clipper

One significant car maker to produce a microcar was Sydney Allard, who, before World War II, had achieved respect as a racing and rally driver.

Although sales of Allard sports cars had been mainly buoyant, sales began to decline during the early 1950s as mainstream car makers returned to full production and began satisfying home-market demand. The venture into the economy market was seen as one way of keeping the factory productive.

Allard's venture with microcars began in 1953 when the Powerdrive company was seeking to manufacture a three-wheeled car designed by David Gottlieb. Known as the Clipper, the small Allard was built using a variety of tried and tested

---

Sydney Allard 1910–1966

Sydney Allard learnt to ride a motorcycle at the age of fourteen. After leaving public school at Ardingly in Sussex, Allard joined W F Lucas Ltd, a Daimler dealership. Motor sport became his passion when he acquired a Grand Prix Morgan three-wheeler, and in 1929 he established his own garage business in Putney. Allard took on a Ford distributorship, and during the 1930s he became well known for a number of Ford-engined trials cars; serious production of these did not materialize because of the outbreak of war.

In 1945 with capital of £100, Sydney Allard established the Allard Motor Co., which evolved as one of Britain's most respected specialist sports cars manufacturers. In 1952, driving his own P Type saloon, Allard won the coveted Monte Carlo Rally. A move into the economy car market was made in 1955 with the Clipper, twenty-two examples being built.

Soon after Sydney Allard's death in 1966, the Allard factory was virtually destroyed by fire.

components, such as a Villiers 346cc engine, Morris Minor brake assemblies and Burman steering and gearbox. The chassis was a cross-braced affair with a single wheel at the front and the engine and gearbox ahead of and driving the rear left-hand wheel. Bodywork for the Clipper was entrusted to the Hordern-Richmond company, who were specialists in the manufacture of fibreglass products at a time when the material was quite novel.

As might be expected of a company experienced in motor sport, the Clipper demonstrated styling that was streamlined to the extent that it was curvaceous and flowing in the extreme. In common with other microcars of the era, the Clipper was equipped with few controls, instruments or luxuries. Built as a saloon it nevertheless lacked side windows, which at least facilitated hand signalling (there were no direction indicators), but side curtains were available for use in wet weather. Essentially a two-seater, a single door was provided on the passenger side only; an unusual feature in minicar design was the adoption of an optional 'dickey' seat at the rear that could accommodate two children.

Raymond Way, the London motor dealer, expressed an interest in selling the Clipper because he was already an agent for Allard as well as being an Allard owner. In fact, Raymond Way was one of the first customers to buy a Clipper when he acquired an example for his wife. Production of Clippers was short-lived despite Allard's advertising, which marketed the car as 'The family car with the lowest running cost'. Allard's claim of 70mpg (4ltr/100km) and joy for five people at a penny a mile can be viewed with period nostalgia. Allard had initially contracted to build 100 Clippers, but problems with supplies of bodies exacerbated the car's demise after only some twenty-two cars had been produced.

As for David Gottlieb, he went on to design the Powerdrive and Coronet three-wheeler sports cars. Both models featured stylish coachwork, but while certainly very small really cannot be classed as microcars.

AC Petite – Made a Little Better than it Need Be . . .

The emergence of a microcar from one of the oldest and most respected sporting marques in automotive history might come as some surprise. However, AC was building three-wheeled vehicles as early as 1903, and by the early 1950s was well known for its invalid cars, production of which continued well into the 1970s, by which time the company shared development and technology with rival Invacars Ltd. In 1953 the company introduced the Petite as a commercially available model to satisfy the demand for economical minicars.

The popularity of the Bond and announcement of the Reliant car in 1952 added to the belief that AC should be enjoying a share of the minicar market. At the opposite end of the motor-car industry to that of Bond and Reliant, AC's early post-war models were viewed as being highly sophisticated, and rivalled such cars as the Jaguar Mark V, Armstrong-Siddeley Typhoon, and the Bristol 400 and 401. As Allard had found, it was essential to keep the factory in full production at a time when austerity still existed to some extent.

From the outset of production the Petite was always a step ahead of its rivals in terms of build quality and comfort over sheer economy. Car-type controls and a column-mounted gear selector were incorporated into the specification, and the whole concept of the AC was superior when compared with the majority of other minicars.

That the AC enjoyed a 'Warren Street elegance' was one way in which a contemporary leading auto magazine described the car. (Warren Street, running parallel to the Euston Road and between Great Portland Street and Tottenham Court Road, was where many colourful motor traders collected to buy and sell many of the prestigious makes of motor car.) The same journal somewhat patronisingly went on to mention that: 'It is a vehicle conceived for the genteel and sedate market formed by those whose preference is for a small four-wheeler, but whose pockets are not deep enough to shoulder the heavy running costs which even small-car ownership entails.'

AC Cars, synonymous with prestigious sports car manufacture, marketed the Petite three-wheeler in 1953. The car shown here is the Mark 2, identifiable as such by the fact that all three wheels are the same size. Mark 1 Petites were fitted with 457mm (18in) spoked wheels at the rear and an 203mm (8in) type at the front. (National Motor Museum)

AC

The fortunes of AC began early in the twentieth century when John Weller and John Portwine established their motor business at West Norwood in South London. Weller was a gifted young engineer and Portwine a respected businessman who owned a chain of butchers' shops. Weller's initial ideas for a 20bhp touring car were deemed too ambitious, and instead he designed, on Portwine's suggestion, a 636cc three-wheeled, wooden-framed delivery vehicle. Known as the Auto-Carrier, it was priced at £85 and sold well.

When the Auto-Carrier Sociable was introduced in 1907 the now recognizable AC trademark was adopted. Sociables proved to be popular and performed outstanding service for their owners. In 1911 AC moved to Thames Ditton in Surrey. A four-wheeled car was introduced before the onset of war in 1914; throughout World War I AC produced armaments.

After the war Selwyn Edge joined AC as a director and in 1921 was appointed Governing Director. Under Edge's directorship AC cars established a number of records, not least that in 1922 a 1,500cc car was the first of its type to cover 100 miles in under an hour. Four years later, an AC won the Monte Carlo Rally for Britain for the first time.

AC cars went into liquidation in 1930 and when the remains of the company were sold off it was brothers William and Charles Hurlock who bought the name. Their intention was to profit from AC's highly successful servicing enterprise, but ultimately they were encouraged back into manufacturing and continuing the AC marque. AC (Scotland) Ltd took over the company in 1984, selling to C P Autokraft Ltd in 1986. Presently the company is registered as AC Cars Group Ltd, but in June 2002 it went into administration. However, with the announcement of new funding, the future for AC appears assured.

Announced in the autumn of 1952, the Petite went on sale the following spring at a price of £255 plus purchase tax, which increased the sum to a little under £400. It was powered by a rear-positioned Villiers 346cc single-cylinder, two-stroke engine, which was rubber-mounted along with the three-speed gearbox and differential so as to achieve as smooth running as possible. An integral chassis and body frame supported aluminium body panels, and the saloon-type cabin with its fabric sunroof provided much more comfort than otherwise might have been expected from such a vehicle.

The wheel arrangement of the Petite, which was unusual to say the least, comprised a layout having two large (18in) spoked types at the rear and a smaller (8in) wheel at the front. In view of AC's experience with invalid carriage design this is understandable. The single front wheel was suspended by two coil springs, and the independently coil-sprung rear wheels were additionally controlled by direct-action dampers. What happened in the event of a puncture remains a mystery, especially as the car was not equipped with a spare wheel of either size. The primary drive to the gearbox was by a V-belt, and the final drive by chain.

The Petite instantly won approval from a discerning clientele, despite having a price tag only a few pounds less than that for which a Ford Popular could be purchased. As far as the specification was concerned, few minicars at the time could boast having such a comfortable interior, with its well-upholstered bench seat and proper doors, not to mention coachwork crafted by professionals more used to building some of the most highly revered sports cars in the world.

The Mark 2 Petite was announced in the autumn of 1955 with the latest Villiers 28B 353cc two-stroke engine. Girling hydraulic brakes were specified on the rear wheels, and the

As might be expected of a product from one of the world's most respected car builders, the Petite, whilst relatively inexpensive to purchase and run, was more luxuriously appointed than most other minicars. Whereas some models had obvious motorcycle or motor scooter connections, the Petite's controls and instruments were thoroughly car-like. (Gordon Fitzgerald)

suspension provided a soft and comfortable ride, even if contemporary test reports did criticize some leaning on corners at higher speeds. Performance was generally more than adequate for a car of its type, and the brakes acted generously despite operating on the rear drums only. In revising the wheel arrangement, AC had adopted common-size pressed steel discs to carry 4×12in tyres.

It can be supposed from contemporary reports, as well as from various subsequent reminiscences, that the Petite was noted for its reliability. Although it was a lot more comfortable and refined than some other minicars of the era, it was still somewhat austere. Lacking a heater, winter driving meant wearing warm clothing, but to put this in its correct context, few popular cars at that time were equipped with heaters. When John Bolster tested the Petite for *Autosport* magazine he found the car to be exceptionally comfortable and spacious, with impressive performance. From his comments about the car not having any tendency to lift a wheel when cornered briskly, it is clear that Bolster obviously enjoyed putting the machine through its paces.

Production of the Petite continued until 1958, by which time falling sales meant that the car had become uneconomical to build. Competition from Reliant and to some extent Bond had taken its toll on the AC and the makers concentrated on supplying three-wheelers as invalid cars. In total, some 4,000 Petites were built, and today, sadly, only a few have survived.

The AC Acedes invalid car, which shared some styling similarities with the Petite, was nonetheless completely different in concept. Driven by a Villiers 197cc engine, it was a single-seater with a single door and had the most basic level of equipment. Between 1957 and 1967, when a new Acedes was introduced, in excess of 15,000 invalid vehicles were manufactured. The new model, distinguishable by its forward-raked rear window and luggage carrier positioned on the engine cover, accounted for some 6,000 sales.

AC did not entirely lose touch with the economy car market after the Petite's demise. The company went on to develop a new three-wheeler which had more than a passing resemblance to the Reliant Regal as well as the Bond 875 but was never put into production. A four-wheeled minicar was also proposed in the early

Petite Mark 2

Chassis

Type	Welded light-gauge steel structure integral with body

Engine

Layout	Villiers air-cooled two-stroke
Peak power	8.25bhp @ 3,500rpm
Bore×stroke	75×80mm
Cubic capacity	353cc

Electrical

Battery	12V
Generator	Lucas dynamo
Starter	Villiers flywheel magneto ignition

Transmission

Gearbox	Burman gearbox with steering-column control; three speeds and reverse

Brakes

Type	Girling hydraulic on rear

Suspension

Front	Trailing link front forks of AC design controlled by coil springs
Rear	Springing by swinging arms, large diameter springs and hydraulic dampers

Tyres

Type	4×12in

Capacity

Fuel tank	13.6ltr (3gal)

Dimensions

Length	3,124mm (10ft 3in)
Width	1,397mm (4ft 7in)
Wheelbase	1,829mm (6ft 0in)
Rear track	1,219mm (4ft 0in)
Weight	836lb (379kg)

Performance

Top speed	49mph (78.9km/h)
Fuel consumption	50mpg (5.7ltr/100km)

AC built invalid carriages that were single-seaters powered by Villiers 197cc engines. (Gordon Fitzgerald)

1970s, and this bore some similarity to Reliant's four-wheeled Kitten. Happily both prototypes have survived.

The Mighty Atom

When World War II hero Air Vice-Marshal Donald 'Pathfinder' Bennett established his car-manufacturing business in the sleepy Buckinghamshire town of Chalfont St Peter in 1954, it was the Fairthorpe Atom that was the issue.

As might be expected from one who was familiar with aircraft principles, the styling of the Atom was aerodynamic in the extreme. Hailed as a sporting bubblecar, the Atom was powered by a rear-mounted BSA 250cc motorcycle engine installed in a steel backbone chassis with a plywood floor. Standard Eight front suspension and steering assembly was used, but instead of employing proprietary rear suspension, Bennett designed this himself. The bodywork was constructed using fibreglass, and surviving images of the prototype vehicle show it having wheel arches that were virtually enclosed both front and rear.

When the Atom went into production it was with a somewhat restyled body. Evident was a lower roofline, headlamps that were incorporated into the tops of the wings, slightly more pronounced wheel arches and rear quarter windows. As with many microcars of the period the Atom failed to attract customers in any numbers; information regarding production is scant to say the least, and it can be presumed that fewer than sixty were sold. Of particular interest is that Donald

Chalfont St Peter in Buckinghamshire is where Air Vice-Marshal Donald Bennett built his Fairthorpe Atom. The name Atom summons the image of a powerful sports car, rather than this minute offering with its BSA 250cc engine. This rather poor quality picture originates from a Fairthorpe sales brochure from around 1954. (National Motor Museum)

Bennett was intent on selling the Atom in America, and the first twenty or so cars that were built at Chalfont St Peter were exported there.

Before production of the Atom ended in 1956, Fairthorpe attempted to introduce a number of technical improvements and modifications. More significant was the adoption of a differential that meant that a tighter turning circle was possible. Hence some of the later cars were seen with full wheel arches at the front. In order to attract a greater number of customers, Fairthorpe introduced two new microcars, the Atom convertible, of which a sole example was built, and the Atomota coupé. The latter was afforded some almost bizarre styling courtesy of an Atom bodyshell complete with a facelifted front end and rear wings that adopted massive fins. The interior, however, was more comfortable. Fairthorpe promoted the Atomota as a performance machine, which it was to the extent that its 650cc BSA twin, now positioned at the front, could propel it to 60mph (100km/h). Few Atomotas were sold, and in any event the introduction of the variant had come about as a result of the need to use up unsold stocks of Atom components and bodyshells. As for Fairthorpe, the company went on to produce some highly respected specialist sports cars, among which were the Electron, Zeta and the TX range of cars.

Bond – Big Cars in Miniature

Lawrie Bond and the Bond Minicar have been discussed at length in Chapter 3, but Bond himself, in addition to the Equipe sports cars, did become involved in the design of two four-wheeled microcars during the 1950s. Bond had been commissioned by Berkeley Coachwork Ltd to design a small sports car, which became known as the Berkeley and was marketed by the newly established Berkeley Cars Ltd of Biggleswade in Bedfordshire. Despite the Berkeley having a 322cc vertical twin Anzani engine, this elegant machine, as small as it was, really is beyond the scope of this book.

At about the same time that Lawrie Bond had been involved with Berkeley he was approached by Opperman to design for them a small economy car with 'big car comfort'. Opperman was a commercial vehicle manufacturer specializing in tractors, and the company foresaw a potential to build and market a range of microcars. Two vehicles were initially envisaged, the two-door Unicar and the Stirling sports coupé.

When it was introduced at the 1956 London Motor Show, the Unicar had the distinction of being the cheapest car then available. Bond had designed the Unicar to use a fibreglass bodyshell mounted on an aluminium alloy tubular subframe. He decided to use the same 322cc Anzani vertical twin that he had specified for the Berkeley, which was positioned at the rear driving the close-set rear wheels through a three-speed gearbox and solid axle (without a differential) with trailing arms.

In terms of comfort the Unicar was in fact quite spartan, with provision of simple hammock front seats. Even more austere were the rear seats, which in fact were no more than padded lids giving access to the engine compartment, battery and toolbox. Those customers who were attracted to the Unicar found the engine prone to overheating, and may have been disappointed that the vehicle lacked the comfort that was sug-gested in its advertising. Sales of the Unicar amounted to some 200 cars, and a number of these were sold in kit form to customers who were sufficiently competent to build the vehicle themselves.

The Stirling – 'New in concept, new in design and new in construction' – was introduced in time for the 1958 London Motor Show. Unicar had anticipated that its Family Speed saloon with its 424cc Excelsior engine, wider rear track and a differential might have sold well and attracted a discerning clientele. The Stirling never did reach production, and in 1959 Opperman abandoned motor car production.

Out of the Frying Pan . . .

Two of Britain's more unusual minicars introduced at about the same time as AC launched its Petite were the Gordon and the Pashley.

The Gordon was a product of Vernons Industries, a company that had a high profile as a manufacturer of invalid carriages, which were known as Vi-Cars. The Vernons name was also familiar to those thousands who completed their football coupons weekly in the hope of winning the jackpot. That the three-wheeler Gordon had styling similarities to the Reliant Regal there is little doubt, but that is where any resemblance ended mechanically. Having a split windscreen and a simple hood affording adequate weather protection, the car was introduced in 1954 at a price well under £300, thus making it the cheapest car in Britain at the time.

The proven 197cc Villiers 8E two-stroke provided the Gordon's means of propulsion. Unlike the Bond which had its engine mounted above the single front wheel, the Gordon's engine was mounted on the off-side of the car ahead of the rear wheel. Transmission was by chain, which meant that there was no provision for a driver's door, a single door being provided on the off-side of the car. The gearbox was a three-speed affair with reverse, and the chassis was constructed as a tubular backbone formed from 50mm (2in) 12-gauge steel. The front wheel was carried on a motorcycle-type bottom-link front fork and a

Having similar styling to the Mark 1 Reliant Regal, the Gordon was built by Vernons Industries, a company more readily known for its football coupons and Vi-Car invalid carriages. (Gordon Fitzgerald)

Similarly to the Bond Family models, the Gordon accommodated two adults and a couple of children. Shown to good effect here is the Villiers 197cc engine, which was fitted to the off-side of the vehicle and drove the corresponding wheel by chain mechanism. (Gordon Fitzgerald)

This idyllic family scene might suggest that the Gordon was more luxuriously finished and equipped than it actually was. Note the wide-opening door for ease of access and the car-type wheels. (Gordon Fitzgerald)

conventional car-type steering head. Suspension on the single front wheel used 'Metalstick' torsion bushes, while the rear suspension comprised independent trailing arms with coil springs.

In performance, the Gordon made good use of the limited power available and top speed was around 40mph (65km/h); fuel consumption varied, and according to contemporary road tests was between 70–94mpg (4–3ltr/100km), according to driving conditions.

The level of finish was not the Gordon's better point: *Motor Cycling* magazine complained of windscreen-wiper leads trailing across the screen; holes in the floor accommodating the pedals letting in too many draughts (a heater was

available for 30s extra); and the single door being too narrow, leaving the less agile with some difficulty in getting in and out of the car.

The Pashley was another Villiers-powered three-wheeler that was introduced in the spring of 1954. W R Pashley Ltd of Chester Street, Birmingham, made light commercial vehicles, 'stop-me-and-buy-ones', rickshaws and ultra-lightweight pick-ups. The company believed it could penetrate the market that the Bond Minicar enjoyed.

The Pashley used the same Villiers engine as the Gordon which was installed at the front so that the single wheel and final drive all formed a sprung unit. The wheels were of 350mm (14in) diameter, which gave the vehicle a more

The Gordon's chassis and running gear.

substantial appearance than actually was the case. Of rectangular shape, the chassis was of welded construction with transverse tubes in bridge formation. In similar fashion to some other minicars the body panels were formed from light alloy. To facilitate ease of maintenance, the Pashley's bonnet panels disconnected from each other by nothing more complicated than Oddie quick-action fasteners that were extensively used in aircraft construction. Each fastener had a slotted head and could be undone with a coin, and when the panels were detached the engine and transmission assembly was completely exposed.

Owing to the Pashley's design of coachwork there was no need for such refinements as doors, although a simple hood kept out the worst of the weather. According to contemporary press releases there were intentions to improve the design and to introduce greater sophistication to the Pashley; several colour schemes were intended, including cream with red upholstery, and the price is listed as being £265 including purchase tax. The Pashley, however, is among those minicars to have fallen into obscurity before it had a chance to prove itself, and as far as is known very few vehicles were produced, and none is known to have survived.

When a Gordon embarked on a run between Land's End and John o'Groats fuel consumption averaged at 62.5mpg (4.5ltr/100km). Other road testing had achieved in excess of 70mpg (4ltr/100km). This extract taken from a contemporary sales brochure says it all.

8 Microcars in All but Name

One microcar more than any other has become a familiar and respected sight on roads throughout its native Europe and beyond. It is the Little Mouse, the Fiat 500, the revered successor to the immortal Topolino. It is debatable whether the 500 Nuova should be included in a book of this nature, since the car is arguably relatively conventional. Minuscule it certainly is, but that did not deter almost a million sales between 1957 and 1975. The concept of the little 500 lived on for successive generations in the guise of the 126, and is manifested in the new generation Cinquecento and Seicento models.

The introduction of the Fiat 500 Nuova was in response to a number of factors. The demise of the Topolino had given rise to the Fiat 600, a car of almost identical proportions but having a modern image, especially with its unitary construction, accommodation for four passengers and their luggage along with a water-cooled, rear-mounted four-cylinder engine and four-speed transmission layout. For many Italian families who wanted a car that was less expensive, smaller and more economical, some microcars then in vogue were simply too austere and were considered not sufficiently robust to cater for the average Latin motorist's driving habits. Thus was born the loveable, go-anywhere, frugal and very petite 500 Nuova.

Curvy, cuddly and cute. The Fiat 500 Nuova's ancestry can be traced to the pre-war Topolino. With its vertical 479cc air-cooled, twin-cylinder engine in the tail, the Cinquecento offered accommodation for two adults and two children. A small compartment under the bonnet afforded some luggage capacity. (Fiat)

A Design is Born

When Dante Giacosa designed the 500 Nuova he was influenced by some of the microcars emerging from different European countries. The Vespa motor scooter had instilled some ideas into his mind, but, more essentially, a young engineer working under his direction displayed some highly interesting ideas for a tiny car using a two-stroke engine. That engineer was Bauhof, whose outline drawings were for a car hardly larger than a bubblecar. Bauhof had conceived the idea for a car having a two-stroke engine positioned directly above the rear wheels to afford as much interior space-saving as possible. Giacosa was not impressed with two-stroke engines, and, preferring four-strokes, concluded that a twin–cylinder version would be a realistic proposition. One possibility would have been a horizontally-opposed type, but ultimately it was an air-cooled vertical twin that was selected. In addition, such a car had to be very affordable, which meant sacrificing some comforts usually associated with bigger models, and it had to be cheap to run.

Before World War II, Fiat's design team had been committed to developing a minicar that was to have been known as the 400. This might have been the eventual successor to the Topolino had war not intervened. Like the Topolino, it was designed as a four-wheeled two-seater, Giacosa having a firm dislike of three-wheelers. The concept of the 400 was rekindled post-war, and the emergence of a prototype in 1953, which had much to do with Bauhof's ideas, resulted in a scale model showing a diminutive vehicle with a rounded shape and much smaller dimensions than those of the original Topolino.

Development of the 500 had reached a critical stage by the autumn of 1954, when Giacosa was presented with some specific design parameters by Fiat directors. The weight of the car had to be kept below 370kg (816lb); a top speed of 53mph (85km/h) had to be possible, and the fuel consumption had to be kept below 4.5ltr/100km. A feature of the car was its roll-back fabric sun roof and the absence of anything other than the most basic interior trim. In January 1956 the go-ahead was given to produce the car, which meant it

Fiat Nuova 500	
Chassis	
Type	Unitary construction
Engine	
Layout	Air-cooled two-cylinder in-line ohv
Peak power	13bhp @ 4,000rpm
Bore×stroke	66×70mm
Cubic capacity	479cc
Compression ratio	6.55:1
Electrical	
Battery	12V, 32amp/h
Transmission	
Clutch	Single dry-plate
Gearbox	Four-speed and final drive combined
Brakes	
Type	Hydraulic; drums; parking brake acting on rear wheels
Suspension	
All-round	Independent front and rear with telescopic shock absorbers
Front	Wishbones and transverse leaf
Rear	Semi-trailing arms and coil springs
Steering	
Type	Worm and sector
Turning circle	8,534mm (28ft)
Tyres	
Type	490×12
Dimensions	
Length	2,969mm (9ft 7¾in)
Width	1,320mm (4ft 3½in)
Wheelbase	1,841mm (5ft 11¾in)
Track	Front: 1,122mm (3ft 7¾in); rear: 1,134mm (3ft 8¼in)
Weight	1,035lb (473kg)
Performance	
Top speed	53mph (85km/h)
Fuel consumption	65mpg (4.4ltr/100km)

going into production in the spring of 1957. The car had acquired a name, too, the 500 Nuova.

Fiat had anticipated introducing the 500 at the Geneva show in early 1957 but failed to meet the deadline; there were two further opportunities, a summer launch, or to wait until the Turin show in November. Fiat chose to unveil its 'Great Little Auto' in the summer with a series of spectacular events at various cities around Italy.

Although it was marketed as a family car, the 500 in reality accommodated two adults and a couple of children with space under the bonnet for some luggage. To put the little Fiat in its proper context, it was considerably smaller than either the Bond Minicar or the Reliant Regal, and it was only a couple of inches longer than the Messerschmitt. Being only some 610mm (2ft) longer than the Isetta bubblecar, it nevertheless afforded big-car comfort. Rather than the Isetta bubble, it should in all fairness be equated with the Isetta 600, the two cars sharing similar vital statistics.

That the 500 provided a measure of independence to thousands of Italian families is understood; however, it was marketed as a young person's car, appealing to female motorists especially who enjoyed the car's styling charms and easy manoeuvrability. Being a car that could be parked in the smallest spaces, the 500 became the essential fashionable town car. Early 500s were bereft of even the most basic comfort aids, such as wind-down or sliding windows. The fixed glasses were considered adequate since the front quarterlights could be opened and the sunroof rolled back. Exterior trim was pared to the absolute minimum and brightwork was limited to the simple bumpers. Even wheel hubcaps were dispensed with in the interest of economy.

The 500 Grows Up

In addition to the saloon, the Giardiniera estate car was offered, which afforded much more in the way of accommodation and carrying capacity. In providing an increased load capacity and flat load area, Fiat engineers had cleverly turned the upright twin on its side so that it laid flat beneath the rear floor. The Giardiniera was heavier than the saloon, and the increased carrying capacity meant that a larger engine of 499.5cc was necessary.

In 1960 Fiat introduced the 500D with the 499.5cc engine. Minor external styling modifications distinguished the car from its predecessor, but it was the interior that displayed some welcome changes. The front luggage compartment was slightly enlarged due to the reshaping of the fuel tank, and the rear seat was made to fold, thereby enhancing the car's luggage capacity still further. By 1961 a windscreen washer was standard equipment, although the car still lacked the luxury of a fuel gauge, the only low-fuel warning being an illuminated indicator on the minimal facia.

Significant changes occurred in March 1965 when the 500F made its debut. Gone were the rear-hinged 'suicide' doors in favour of the front-hinged type, the drive shafts were modified, and a new and stronger clutch and differential were fitted. The 500L was introduced in 1968 when the Fiat was given new instrumentation, replacing the earlier tiny binnacle, to incorporate a fuel gauge. The last of the 500s was the 500R, which sported a truly more energetic air-cooled twin of 594cc. This, incidentally, was the power unit that was used to drive the boxy 126, the 500's successor.

In time, the 126 was replaced by the 126 Bis, a Polish-built Fiat with a water-cooled engine. This model was the ultimate in baby Fiats at the time and was, in comparison to those cars introduced in 1957, quite luxurious, especially with its opening tailgate and laid-flat engine, both combining to provide a hatchback style of car.

A Micro People Carrier

Belonging to a different category of Fiats was the Multipla, a vehicle having few connections with the latter-day model of the same name. Based on the Fiat 600 platform, the Multipla was in effect a first-generation people carrier. Constructed on an integral chassis no larger than that of the original Topolino's, the Multipla could accommodate

The 500 was launched in the summer of 1957. Early examples were pared to the minimum in the interest of economy. There was a minimum of brightwork and the only windows that opened were the front quarterlights, hence the need for a fabric sunroof. (Fiat)

In addition to the saloon, Fiat marketed an estate car, the Giardiniera. The 499.5cc engine was laid on its side and tucked under the floor of the car.

The 500D was introduced in 1960. The suicide doors were retained along with minimal instrumentation. Modifications over previous models included adoption of the 499.5cc engine, a folding rear seat and increased luggage space under the bonnet.

Fiat 500 Chronology

- Nuova introduced in the summer of 1957 with a 479cc engine. Production: 181,036.

- The 500D, having an engine enlarged to 499.5cc, made its debut in 1960 and remained in production until 1965. 640,520 cars were built.

- 500F announced in March 1965 with some extensive styling revisions. 499.5cc engine retained.

- 500L made its appearance in 1968 and was virtually identical to the 500F apart from minor revi-

sions. Both cars remained in production until 1972. Combined output accounted for 2,272,092 vehicles.

- 500R built from 1972–75. Engine enlarged to 594cc, but otherwise the interior trim was similar to the 500F. 334,000 cars produced.

- 126 in production from 1973–92; 126 fitted with air-cooled 594cc engine, 126 Bis with 704cc water-cooled unit. Production of all 126 cars: 80,868.

A line-up of 500s of varying age. In excess of 3,427,000 Nuovas were built between 1957 and 1975. Today, 500s enjoy a hugely enthusiastic following.

six people on three rows of seats. The power to propel this miniature gargantuan was the 600's 633cc four-cylinder, water-cooled unit. Featuring a rear-mounted engine and transmission, the exceptional carrying capacity was achieved by adopting a single-box body with forward control so that the driver and front passenger sat directly above the front wheels.

The Multipla quickly became a firm favourite throughout Europe, serving as taxicabs,

Regarded as being the first true people-carrier, the Fiat Multipla accommodated six or seven people in a vehicle the length of the Fiat 600. (Tony Spillane)

ambulances and delivery vehicles with aplomb. The Multipla was easily thirty years ahead of its time when it was introduced at the Brussels Motor Show in January 1956. Families, too, opted to buy the Multipla, for it doubled as a camping van as well as transportation for larger tribes. In Watford, north of London, a fleet of Multiplas served as taxis over a number of years. Sadly, few Multiplas have survived.

Fiat 500s Abroad

Three marques in particular benefited from Fiat 500 Nuova influence. One was the Autobianchi; the others were NSU and Abarth.

The Bianchina was the first car to emerge from a union between Bianchi, Fiat and Pirelli. A standard Fiat 500-based car was introduced in the autumn of 1957 and eleven months later the Bianchina Speciale made its entrance, with an engine that was developed for the Fiat 500 in sporting guise. These really were microcars with big hearts, the Speciale having lowered suspension and a trim that was, by 500 Nuova standards, quite luxurious. The Autobianchi was neatly designed with a trim body, and the Speciale

featured both coupé and convertible styling. The latter was always rare in right-hand-drive form, and today even left-hand-drive models are extremely difficult to find. Fiat running gear was adopted throughout the range of models, which were sought by those motorists who favoured Fiat's engineering but wanted more in the way of performance and style than the standard 500 could offer.

More functional was the Autobianchi van with its promising load capacity and full-height tailgate. Similarly to the Fiat 500 Giardiniera, the Autobianchi van had its engine lying flat under the rear floor to afford 10cu m (35cu ft) carrying space.

A Noddy Car

The smallest Fiat sharing the platform of the 500 Nuova was the coach-built roadster by Vignale of Turin. With styling not dissimilar to the car depicted in Enid Blyton's children's stories, along with the fact that many examples were painted red and yellow, it is not surprising that these delectable little vehicles became known as Noddy cars.

Ideas were sketched for a new 500 and ultimately this proposal was used for the Autobianchi. (Fiat)

The Bianchina Special had Fiat 500 running gear and relatively luxurious trim. Lower suspension than that fitted to the Fiat afforded a flatter ride.

The Bianchina convertible is now a rare item. This car is owned by D.P. Motors.

Vignale of Turin produced this tiny derivative of the Fiat 500. Known as the Gamine, it was more often referred to as a Noddy car.

Multiplas were constructed by specialist coachbuilders, in addition to those built by Fiat. This is the Coriasco version, which had seats that folded away to afford an unequalled load area accessed by double doors on the driver's side. By adopting forward control and positioning the engine at the rear, maximum interior space was obtained.

Known as the Gamine, Vignale's demure offering rekindled the fabled Fiat Balilla sports cars of the 1930s. A feature of the Gamine was its huge dummy radiator at the front. In common with the Fiat 500 Nuova, the Gamine of course had the by-now established air-cooled twin in its tail. Unlike the Fiat 500, or indeed some of the other more significant microcars of the era, the Gamine was arguably rather impractical, and as a result did not sell in large numbers.

Mostly built with left-hand drive, a few right-hand-drive Gamines were imported into Britain by Demetriou & Sons and commanded a price of around £700, which in most instances was considered to be too expensive. Those Gamines that have survived are cherished by their owners and have now become collectors' items.

Another coach-built variant of repute was the Fiat 500 Jolly, a fun car and beach buggy built by Ghia. The Jolly was at home on both the French

---

Vignale

Carrozzeria Vignale was established in Turin in 1945 by Alfredo Vignale, who had been apprenticed to the coachbuilding industry, and who had acquired much respect while working for Farina. The company specialized in creations for Alfa Romeo, Lancia and Fiat, as well as producing coachwork for Cisitalia and Siata. Alfredo Vignale died in November 1969 when he was involved in a road accident; Alejandro de Tomaso acquired the company, and the Vignale coachworks was used to build specialist Ford cars. The Vignale name is now owned by Ford.

---

and Italian Riviera, or in California. Built without weather protection and featuring wicker seats, the Jolly was not a practical city car.

The NSU Factor

NSU–Fiat cars were built at Heilbronn for the German market; in 1959, owing to a legal dispute, the company changed its name to Neckar. Fiat had bought NSU's manufacturing plant at Heilbronn in 1930 to satisfy local demand, and two cars to be built there during the 1950s and 1960s were the Weinsberg 500 limousette and coupé. Both cars were fitted with Fiat 500 Nuova running gear, but the coachwork was entirely different to that of the Italian car. The trim, too, was different, and in contrast to the Fiat 500's stark interior it was remarkably luxurious.

A Sporting Micro

Abarth, that highly respected name in sporting circles, is virtually synonymous with Fiat. Known for its powerful adaptations of Fiat running gear, at the Turin Show in the autumn of 1957 Abarth displayed a 500 that was capable of speeds in excess of 62mph (100km/h).

When the 500D made its debut, Abarth responded by introducing the 595 with a 594cc engine capable of producing 27bhp and a top speed of 75mph (120km/h). The 695 followed with a power plant of 689cc and 90mph

(145km/h). Fiat 500 Abarths are a familiar sight on the world's racing circuits, and it is remarkable what can be achieved from such a tiny motor car.

Microcars from the Land of the Rising Sun

A number of microcars have emerged from Japan, some of which have taken the minicar concept to the far edge of technology, while others have been relatively conventional but parcelled into tiny packages.

An example of the latter is the Subaru 360, which was launched a year after the Fiat 500 Nuova. Having a 356cc two-stroke twin fitted in the tail, the car shared certain similarities with its Latin cousin, but was otherwise remarkable by virtue of its odd styling. Popular in its native Japan, Subaru exported the 360 to Europe and America, where it failed to sell in any significant numbers. The 360 has now achieved a cult status and surviving examples are keenly sought by microcar enthusiasts.

Honda is another high-profile name, the company establishing its motor car building in 1962. Among the first models to appear was the S360 sports car fitted with the same 356cc twin-ohc, four-cylinder engine that was fitted to the little Honda truck. In 1968 Honda introduced the 354cc N360 saloon in answer to Japan's motor tax arrangements, which favoured cars having engines smaller than 360cc.

Suzuki produced a microcar as early as 1955, when the company introduced the Suzulight, which had a two-stroke, twin-cylinder engine of 360cc capacity. A series of Suzulights emerged until the Fronte appeared in 1967 with an air-cooled, three-cylinder two-stroke.

Mazda arrived on the scene in 1960 with a microcar designated the R–360. The engine was an air-cooled V-twin, and although performance was modest, Japan's motorists liked the car and in excess of 23,000 were sold in its first year of manufacture. A tiny coupé, the R–360 was not unlike the NSU Weinsberg, and despite such a modest engine the car nevertheless reached speeds above 55mph (89km/h).

Fiat 500 technology was used for the NSU Weinsberg.

The Japanese Subaru 360 was introduced in 1958 and had a rear-mounted 356cc twin two-stroke engine. The car has now achieved cult status in its native country and elsewhere. (Subaru)

Subarus are used in motor sport as depicted here. Trailing is a brace of Trabants. (Subaru)

The Daihatsu Bee was also an instant success when it was introduced in 1954. This was the firm's first car, and, unlike the other Japanese microcars mentioned, this was a three-wheeler with the single wheel at the front. Driven by a 250cc V-twin of 13.5bhp, the Bee was built for a couple of years before Daihatsu abandoned car production until 1962 in order to concentrate on commercial vehicles. As small as it was, the Bee became popular with taxicab operators, who liked the vehicle's minimal running costs. Customers also favoured the Bee – government legislation meant that fares were based on a vehicle's engine size and overall dimensions, so travelling in a Bee was cheaper than it would be in larger cabs.

In Japan, those vehicles having engines of less than 360cc were regarded as K-class motors, and accounted for some 23.4 per cent of that country's domestic car market during the 1950s and 1960s. In addition to the foregoing names, both Toyota and Mitsubishi were contenders in this lucrative market.

9 Breeds Apart

Those makes of vehicle that were perceived to offer more in the way of sophistication than some other minicars and bubblecars did much to enhance the microcar concept. Marques such as the Goggomobil, Janus, Vespa and Frisky made an impact on the minicar scene during the 1950s and 1960s, and they afforded real-car motoring on nothing more than the most frugal of running costs. Along with the aforementioned, the Fuldamobil had a habit of emerging around the world under various guises, and several others that came within the general microcar classification, such as the Australian Lightburn, were instrumental in establishing microcar markets in arguably the least likely countries.

Built by Hans Glas, the Goggomobil is regarded for its build quality and reliability. Models such as the T300, which is illustrated, were built with right-hand drive for the British market.

From Scooters to Microcars

Goggo scooters were first manufactured in 1951 by the Bavarian company Hans Glas GmbH of Dingolfing. Until then, the company was better known for its agricultural machinery. In 1955 Glas ventured into the microcar market with the Goggomobil, a car that quickly became associated with build quality and reliability. The T250 sold well and was replaced by the T300 saloon along with a pretty little coupé that had considerable panache. Glas then entered the commercial market building microvans and trucks, and in 1962 Goggos were additionally built in Spain. BMW acquired Glas in 1966 for DM91 million, and in 1968 production of the Goggomobil was halted. In excess of 280,000 Goggomobils were built, a fine tribute to the car's creator who died at the age of 78 in 1968.

Goggomobil T300

Chassis	
Type	Integral with body
Engine	
Layout	Vertical twin, air–cooled
Peak power	14.8bhp @ 5,000rpm
Bore × stroke	58 × 56mm
Cubic capacity	293cc
Compression ratio	6:1
Transmission	
Gearbox	Constant layshaft; four speeds and reverse
Brakes	
Type	Hydraulic
Suspension	
Type	Swing axle, coil springs front and rear; telescopic hydraulic dampers
Steering	
Type	Rack and pinion
Tyres	
Type	4.40 × 10in
Dimensions	
Length	2,908mm (9ft 6½in)
Width	1,283mm (4ft 2½in)
Wheelbase	1,791mm (5ft 10½in)
Track	Front & rear: 1,086mm (3ft 6¾in)
Weight	8cwt (406kg)
Performance	
Top speed	56.5mph (91km/h)
Fuel consumption	60–65mpg (4.71–4.35ltr/100km)

When the prototype Goggomobil T250 was unveiled it had a single front opening door similar to that of the Iso, Isetta and Heinkel bubblecars. Whereas the BMW Isetta 600 additionally had a side door for rear-seat passengers, the Goggo was not so equipped. In reality the rear seat was intended for children, and as the front seats tipped forwards to afford access to it, the manufacturer appeared not to have had concerns regarding safety or convenience. During the car's gestation period Glas must have had second thoughts about the initial design because when the vehicle went into production two rear-hinged side doors substituted the front opening affair.

The T250 benefited from a spirited performance courtesy of a rear-mounted, air-cooled 14bhp 247cc two-stroke vertical twin engine of Glas design. The T250's weight was kept to an absolute minimum to ensure that the car could easily achieve 50mph (80km/h) and return 50mpg (5.6ltr/100km). Such fuel economy together with the vehicle's ample accommodation attracted many customers; in excess of 25,000 T250s were built between 1955 and the end of 1956.

When the T250 was given more power via a 293cc engine, the model was renamed T300.

When that most highly respected motoring journalist Gordon Wilkins met the Goggo for the first time he found it remarkable that a tiny car could achieve so much. It took seven seconds to reach 30mph (50km/h) from a standing start, and the machine could be flung around corners at astonishing speeds; over cobbles, tracks and across fields, while the Goggo's suspension soaked up the bumps.

The Goggo's transmission was somewhat unconventional, in that it relied not on sliding gears but dog clutches as a means of engagement. Drivers not used to the Goggo could at first be caught out by the transverse movement gear selection with its fore and aft neutral. Having a combined engine, gearbox and final drive, the clutch on the Goggo was fitted between the gearbox and final drive unit, which meant adopting a particular technique when changing between ratios. Only a finger-light touch on the selector lever was required to change gear.

In 1958 improvements were made to the Goggo's interior; with all-round vision being excellent, winding windows replaced the sliding type, and a greater amount of room meant that four adults could be accommodated rather than two adults and a couple of children. The seats themselves were made more comfortable, those at the front collapsing to form a bed when

aligned with the rear-seat cushions. Two-tone paintwork was optional, and inside the car a fresh new trim arrangement was appreciated by prospective customers. When sold in Britain, the T300 was marketed as the Regent, and attracted sales from those customers who wanted a minicar with four wheels rather than three, and which promised more in the way of big-car comfort than could a bubblecar.

Goggomobil Coupé

When it was announced in 1957, the Goggomobil TS300 coupé promised to be a winner among microcars. Goggomobil production was then around 170 vehicles a day but with the new car coming on line, this was stepped up to a daily total of 200, some 30 per cent of output reserved

T300s really did accommodate a family of four in comfort. UK-market cars were known as Regents and provided amazing performance in relation to engine size.

for the coupé. Delightfully styled, the sports Goggo was reminiscent of the Alfa Giulietta, and quite unlike any other vehicle of its size or type.

Viewed as being a 'junior Porsche', the Goggo coupé quickly made a reputation for itself, especially as it had an interior that was markedly more luxurious than that of the saloon's.

Although the basic structure of the coupé remained essentially the same as that of the saloon, a very different feature was the gearbox. Fitted with electric preselection, the Getrag-built box comprised four forward ratios, all indirect, which were formed by constant-mesh gears running on hollow shafts and incorporating a system of bobbins and steel balls. It would appear that a similar principle of operation was debated in respect of the Formula 2 Lotus gearbox, but was ultimately abandoned because the technology used by Getrag applied stress concentrations that were considered too high for racing purposes. The system nevertheless worked well on the Goggo with its modest torque. Gear selection was made via a miniature gear lever on the instrument housing, with a separate selector button for reverse.

Gear changing was effected by kicking down on the clutch pedal; contemporary road-test reports indicate that testers derived much fun from the transmission system as it enhanced the car's sporting characteristics. The coupé's top speed was in excess of 60mph (100km/h), and because the 293cc engine was valveless, it was reputed to be virtually unburstable.

The coupé's front suspension with its divided axle and coil-spring damper struts was similar to that employed on Lotus sports cars. Rear

In the tail of the T300 sat a 247cc air-cooled twin.

Goggos were built as vans in addition to the saloon and a charming little coupé. (Gordon Fitzgerald)

suspension also had Lotus qualities – having a coil spring and damper strut, the rear wheels were located by their drive shafts combined with a rearward-projected radius arm.

Janus – In the Spirit of the Roman God

Of similar proportions to the Goggomobil was the Zündapp Janus, a peculiar two-door bubble-car with openings at either end instead of at the sides. A four-wheeled four-seater, this was the ultimate in extrovert design; the car looked virtually identical from whichever way it was viewed. Employing a 248cc single-cylinder, two-stroke engine, the Janus was introduced in 1957, by which time the Goggomobil and other micro-cars had already commanded a fair share of the minicar market.

With doors at either end stylishly like the front opening of the Isetta, the Janus did not win any prizes in the sociability stakes; front and rear passengers sat with their backs to each other. Between the two sets of seats was positioned the engine, a modified version of the Zündapp motorcycle unit. Despite the car's curious looks it nevertheless performed well with a top speed of almost 53mph (85km/h) and fuel consumption

bettered 52mpg (5.4ltr/100km). The Zündapp was short-lived, as sales fell short of what the makers had anticipated; some 6,000 cars were built before production was abandoned.

Vespa

Being an Italian company and sharing a strong family affinity with the Vespa motor scooter, Piaggio oddly decided not to build the Vespa microcar in its native country. Instead, Piaggio had the car built in France by ACMA at Fourchambault. The car was created in response to Fiat's near domination of the Italian auto market.

Similarly to the Goggomobil, the Vespa represented truly big-car motoring in miniature, and in many respects rivalled the Fiat 500 Nuova, although it failed to sell in such impressive numbers. Side by side, the Vespa and Goggo looked alike and had comparable accommodation and performance. Top speed was 50mph (80km/h) courtesy of an air-cooled vertical twin of 393cc, with 50mpg (5.6ltr/100km) being easily possible. Transmission was via a three-speed gearbox; the tyres were the same size as those specified for the Goggo, and the chassis, too, was integral. Built between 1957 and 1961, the Vespa failed to challenge either the Fiat 500

Vespas vied for the same market as the Goggomobil and Fiat 500. Although of Italian origin, Vespa cars were built in France.

Nuova or the Goggomobil. Nevertheless, some 35,000 examples were sold.

Frisky by Name and Nature

One of the more idiosyncratic microcars to appear was the British-built Frisky. The car's coachwork was styled by one of Italy's most gifted stylists, Giovanni Michelotti, who also penned the Triumph Herald. As was mentioned in Chapter 7, businessman Captain Raymond Flowers had conceived the idea of the Frisky while stationed in Egypt in the mid-1950s. Only when he returned to Britain did Flowers further his microcar concept, in the wake of the Suez crisis. Unable to produce the vehicle himself, Flowers collaborated with

engine maker Henry Meadows to build the car, which by then had evolved from a rather quaint design featuring a single up-and-over door.

The first Frisky was not representative of the definitive car. Looking something like a cross between a Peel and an Isetta, the vehicle with its side-mounted and roof-hinged door managed to compete a marathon week-long, non-stop trial at Oulton Park in early 1957. Meanwhile, Michelotti was finalizing his drawings for the prototype car which was shown at the 1957 Geneva Motor Show. Elegant and with a large glass area, this was a minicar with gull-wing doors that was built by Vignale. Perhaps not surprisingly, Michelotti's styling was considered impractical for a production microcar, even if the car had caused a sensation when shown.

An entirely different Frisky was introduced at the 1957 Earls Court Motor Show. With Michelotti's styling influence evident, there were in fact two designs, the Sport open tourer and a coupé. 'Britain's answer to world demand' was the marketing message, and the car was priced a few shillings under £500, which included purchase tax. Few cars were cheaper at the time except three-wheelers; only four-wheelers such as the Goggomobil and Fairthorpe Atom came within the sub-£500 price range, except for the Ford Popular.

The Frisky's specification was simple – it had an ultra light yet very rigid ladder chassis and a fibreglass body with a separate tail section bonded to it. Building of bodies was initially undertaken by Hill's Fibreglass Developments, but after a short period was entrusted to Guy Motors. On coupé variants the tail section was integral with the main body and ultimately this modification was applied to Sport versions. Both variants had a rear-mounted, air-cooled 249cc Villiers two-stroke parallel twin-cylinder engine along with a motorcycle gearbox and chain final drive. In practice with a number of microcars, the rear wheels were closely set so as to avoid fitting a differential. Hardly had the Frisky gone into production when a larger engine was specified. The Villiers 324cc two-stroke was chosen to produce 16bhp and afford breathtaking performance for a microcar, 65mph (105km/h) being possible along with 55mpg (5ltr/100km) fuel consumption.

While the Frisky was praised for its overall concept it nonetheless attracted some criticism.

UNMATCHED STYLING, COMFORT AND ECONOMY

The Vespa 400 had a two-cylinder, air-cooled engine of 393cc capacity. The car's interior was neatly trimmed and to provide increased luggage capacity the front passenger seat folded forwards. If one were to believe the sales brochure's claims, the car was fitted with air conditioning, which meant that air was warmed via a heat exchanger before entering the cabin.

The Frisky enjoyed a measure of popularity following its introduction in 1957. Promoted by the three Flowers brothers, Raymond, Neville and Derek, the Frisky was built in Wolverhampton courtesy of Henry Meadows (Vehicles) Ltd. The glassfibre bodies were made nearby in the Guy factory. This scene shows cars under varying degrees of construction. (National Motor Museum)

The Frisky coupé may not have appeared to be in the sports league. Nevertheless it did command a good turn of speed and could reach nearly 60mph (100km/h). This 1958 model is seen at Brands Hatch. (National Motor Museum)

Getting in and out of the cabin called for a degree of agility if the driver wanted to avoid clashing shin with steering column, and because the wheels were set well back in line with the leading edges of the 'suicide' doors it meant clambering across the wheel arch. The coupé's removable rigid plastic slide-opening side screens were not as easy to operate as might have been desired, and a road test revealed some rather unwelcome draughts around one's legs.

The Frisky proved to be one of the more successful microcars of the 1950s, with production continuing until 1964. In addition to four-wheeled cars Frisky also produced a three-wheeler which shared styling similarities. This was the Frisky Three with its single wheel trailing and choice of engines, a Villiers 197cc single cylinder or a 250cc twin. The latter was eventually abandoned, and the wheelbase shortened;

the rubber in torsion front suspension was also revised in favour of McPherson struts.

After 1961 production of the Frisky was restricted to three-wheelers. A number of financial difficulties had beset Frisky and the company changed hands on at least three occasions. When the Frisky Three finally went out of production in 1964, the minicar era was virtually at an end.

An Australian Connection

Designs for the Frisky had been adventurous, with some promising plans for a micro sports car. Although prototype vehicles appeared from time to time, few production vehicles were built. The concept did survive however; the Lightburn company of Australia took up the design for its Zeta Sports. Few Zeta Sports were actually sold because when the car was introduced in 1964 the

One of the more obscure microcars as far as the Western hemisphere is concerned, is the Zeta, which was built by the Australian Lightburn company. Functional to the point of being utilitarian, the Zeta was marketed as Australia's own second car.

The Fuldamobil appeared in Britain as the Nobel and was built at Bristol and in Northern Ireland courtesy of Nobel Industries. (Gordon Fitzgerald)

Mini Cooper and other small cars had scooped the market share that microcars had previously enjoyed. Furthermore, vehicle lighting regulations were being introduced in Australia, with which the Zeta Sports did not comply.

Lightburn marketed a range of Australian-built microcars under the Zeta name, and from the outset these were aimed at families wanting a second car. For a country having such a diverse terrain as Australia even a microcar had to be very durable. Officially classified as runabouts, Zetas were viewed as being capable of fulfilling multifunctional roles, as family sedans, station sedans and delivery vehicles. These Zetas featured front-wheel drive and were powered by the Villiers 3STR 324cc air-cooled, two-stroke vertical twin engine. In February 1964 a standard Zeta covered the 1,000 miles between Newcastle and Adelaide non-stop in under 24 hours. The proving run produced an average speed of 44.4mph (71.4km/h) and 41.5mpg (6.8ltr/100km) fuel consumption without any mechanical problems.

When Donald Campbell and the Bluebird team surveyed Lake Eyre, Lightburn Zetas were chosen as support vehicles. Project director and Bluebird relief driver, Andrew Mustard, found the cars' light weight and front-wheel drive indispensable when traversing soft, salt-lake surfaces; the fibreglass bodies were also unaffected by salt corrosion.

A Microcar of Many Coats

Mention has been made earlier of the Fuldamobil with its caravan connections. From its origins in 1951, the Fuldamobil evolved as an egg-shaped microcar that enjoyed a healthy and loyal following. Built in Germany, Holland, Sweden, Norway, Greece, Zimbabwe (previously Southern Rhodesia), Argentina, Chile and the United Kingdom, Fuldamobils in one form or another, and under different names, became a familiar sight around the world. Mostly of three-wheeler concept (trailing rear wheel), but occasionally four (rear wheels closely set to avoid use of a differential), the designs proved to be as diverse as the number of countries of production. Most variants used the Fichtel & Sachs engine, although some employed Heinkel or Ilo units.

Fuldamobils were introduced into Britain in 1958 and were built under licence in England

and Northern Ireland by Nobel Industries. Peter York Nobel had previously been involved with Heinkel and had sensed that the S7 Fuldamobil would sell in quantity. Anticipated sales were ambitious to say the least, and a weekly production of 400 failed to materialize. The Nobel failed to compete with the market that was dominated mainly by Bond and Reliant, together with Isetta, Heinkel and Messerschmitt. In total, around 1,000 were sold, and there are claims that Nobels remained in dealerships long after production was abandoned in 1962.

The Fuldamobil suffered towards the end of its production era because of strong competition from small mass-produced cars including the Japanese 'K' class vehicles. Nevertheless, Fuldamobils under varying guises afforded quality motoring to thousands around the world, and the concept remained until well into the 1970s.

A Treasure from the Czech Republic

There is a charisma about the Velorex that few microcars can match. The concept of this fragile-looking machine dates from 1942 when the Stransky brothers built a vehicle that was designed for use by a disabled person. The basis of the machine was simple, being propelled by an air-cooled Pal 300 engine, and it could be adapted to meet the demands of the owner. Some ten vehicles were eventually constructed, each being unique in that the tubular frame could be extended to provide a larger version than was the norm. The high cost of metal meant that bodies were constructed from a woven waterproof material similar to leather-cloth and stretched over a simple tubular frame. To economize on mechanical items, bicycle components were used where possible.

Anticipating that the Czech people would need an inexpensive means of transportation, the Stransky brothers sought to extend their vehicle business after World War II. Because of the political situation in Czechoslovakia there was little prospect that such a car could be built, unless a decision was forthcoming by the many committees that regulated every aspect of industry and daily life. Only by promoting the vehicle as an invalid car did the enterprise stand any chance of becoming a reality.

Thus the Stransky machines were built in small numbers from 1945. Although quite minimal in design, they were a good deal more sophisticated

The Velorex was built in the Czech Republic and like some other minicars was originally designed as an invalid car. With its lightweight frame and fabric body, the Velorex displayed amazing performance. (Ivana Birkettova)

There may be few Velorex cars in Britain, but elsewhere in Europe they are highly prized. (Ivana Birkettova)

than the invalid cars that had been previously. The Czech government took control of production in 1950 and allocated it to a co-operative known as Velo. By 1953 considerable numbers of three-wheelers were being built as Oskars and were characterized by 16in wheels and Jawa motorcycle technology. A name change occurred in 1954 when the Oskar became known as the Velorex.

Production of the Velorex continued until 1974 and although much development had taken place, the car remained essentially the simple runabout as first designed. Because of its ultra-light weight-to-power ratio, the Velorex enjoyed a rate of acceleration that equalled many a production vehicle. Desperately basic in its construction and appointment, the Velorex nevertheless attracted a loyal clientele. Today, examples of Velorex are extremely sought after, and the associated enthusiast's club is particularly active.

10 The Microcar Revival

During the 1970s the revival in the demand for microcars largely emanated from France where relaxed laws meant that cars under 50cc could be driven by anyone over the age of fourteen. Furthermore, such cars could be used without need of a driving licence, nor was there any requirement to have them tested annually under the matriculation scheme, the equivalent of the British MOT test. In France, as elsewhere in the early 1970s, the fuel crisis brought the necessity for economical motoring to the fore.

An abundance of microcars emerged – most had two seats, basic interiors and minimal equipment. Fibreglass bodies were the norm along with tiny wheels, automatic transmission and minuscule engines that buzzed like bees. Some cars were no more than boxes on wheels, while others featured eccentric styling. The demand for microcars so escalated that they became a familiar sight in rural areas as well as in towns and cities.

The majority of French microcars were four-wheelers, although three-wheelers did achieve some popularity. The microcar theme also spread to the commercial sector with the most diminutive delivery vans and trucks adding a bizarre character to French streets. Some well-established companies such as Vins Nicolas operated minitrucks in Paris and other cities.

Whilst ultra low-powered microcars had obvious advantages, there emerged a demand for larger-engined machines. These had petrol engines of around 125cc, with larger units up to 250cc and 500cc being optional. In the case of the latter there was a risk of losing sales to the almost conventional by comparison Citroën 2CV and Renault 4. Among the more familiar microcars to appear from France were: the

William with its Lambretta connections; Erad; the highly unusual Flipper; Ligier (a name more familiar in motor racing circles); and Aixam.

Microcars were also popular in Italy, where several makes, often as unusual as those in France, were built. None were more peculiar than the triangular-shaped BMA Brio, which really did not appear to be at all practical. For the British, the new wave of microcars was deemed mostly to be too unconventional for the majority of motorists, who were more used to Bonds, Reliants and bubblecars. While demand for such vehicles grew rapidly in other parts of the world, the British market was slow to accept the new concept.

The French take the Lead

Revered both in France and Italy, the William was one of the first of the modern microcars to make a debut. The William was introduced in the mid-1960s at the Paris Salon, and by the middle of the 1970s the marque had become well established. The car took the name of the French Lambretta scooter importer, who visualized that a simple but small economy car would attract a particular niche market. M. William was proved correct, and the cars that were fitted with 125cc or 175cc engines according to choice evoked much interest. In fact, the car was virtually an international affair; having Fiat 500 Nuova suspension, it was built in Italy by Scattolini. Now firmly established, William formed a union with Lambretta to market the cars in Italy as the Lawil.

Erad was among the most respected names in the French microcar industry before it went out of business in 1997. Formed in 1975, production of a wide range of vehicles, which included electric and diesel power as well as petrol, accounted for in excess of 30,000 units. The first Erad cars had 47cc Sachs engines; then came a 290cc diesel-engined machine in addition to a 123cc petrol minicar. For those who wanted an MG in miniature, Erad offered a replica 1936 Midget that was only 2,743mm (9ft) in length and was fitted with either a 600cc diesel or 125cc petrol engine. Later Erads were more conventional-looking than some of the earlier types, with the Spacia of 1990 appearing like a diminutive yet-to-be launched Renault Twingo. When Erad went into liquidation, it was SAVEL that took over production.

When the Flipper was unveiled in 1978 it represented some of the more idiosyncratic ideas that emanated from French microcars of the immediate post-war era. Easy to drive with its two-speed automatic transmission, and even easier to park, the Flipper was constructed by Flipper Sarl of Villejuif. A four-wheeler with narrow-track front wheels and a Sachs 47cc or Motobécane 50cc engine, it could turn through

In recent years microcars have made a steady revival. The French were largely responsible for this with the introduction of miniature cars such as the Erad as seen here. The majority of French micros had engines no larger than 49cc. (Gordon Fitzgerald)

French micros were never more idiosyncratic than the Flipper. The narrow-track front wheels could be turned through 360 degrees. (Gordon Fitzgerald)

360 degrees in similar fashion to the Bond Minicar. The plastic bodywork was unusual in that it comprised two mouldings that were joined together to form a monocoque. Taking up so little space, it was usual to see the tiny Flipper parked at right angles to the pavement. Looking somewhat precarious owing to its size and odd styling, top speed of the Flipper was limited to 25mph (40km/h).

When Ligier announced that it was venturing into the microcar market in addition to being one of the most formidable names in motor sport, success was ensured virtually overnight. The two-seater JS4 featured a 50cc Motobécane engine and automatic transmission. Unlike most other new-generation microcars, Ligiers featured all-metal bodies, and there was independent suspension too. Within a year of its announcement some 7,000 Ligiers had been sold, making this among the most popular of French minicars. Ligier was instrumental in offering diesel engines as standard throughout its range of cars by 1985, and while fibreglass bodywork took over from metal, the cars possessed much in the way of comfort and interior refinement. Ligier believed that microcars should offer more than just basic comfort, and today the company's range of cars is fitted with levels of trim and equipment that would be expected of much larger vehicles.

Similarly to Ligier, Aixam has moved into the

luxury microcar market. Since the company's establishment in 1983, Aixam have specialized in producing microcars that are designed to provide longevity of service and a high degree of reliability. Within four years more Aixams were being sold than any other microcar and had 35 per cent of the market.

In the same vein is Microcar, the company formed in 1980 by boat builders Janneau of Vendée. Microcar has been highly successful thanks in part to an efficient distributor network, but more because the controlling company accepted that French motorists wanted much more in the way of sophistication than had once been the case. Microcar's success was that some 20,000 vehicles were sold in the firm's first seven years of trading, and both Ligier and Aixam vied, along with Microcar, to take the biggest slice of a now lucrative market.

A close look at the French microcar industry shows that the days are over for the buzzing little contraptions that pervaded the roads of France. In many respects this is regrettable because the diverse number of firms building what were essentially throwbacks to the older generation of minicars has largely been reduced to a few specialist concerns.

It is not only the French who have preoccupied themselves with building microcars. A series of concept microcars and prototypes has emerged from Japan, Germany, Italy, America and even Britain. With increasing demands for fuel efficiency and cars that take up less space on crowded roads, it is only to be expected that more work in this line of automotive design will continue.

Microcars Today and Tomorrow

The demand for inexpensive motoring, whether for pleasure or business, has resulted in a diverse range of vehicles that are currently available.

More recent Erads were more car-like and could be obtained with a variety of power sources – petrol, diesel or electric.

Modern micros such as this IDM are comprehensively equipped and offer as much comfort as conventional vehicles.

When Alan Evans introduced his 49cc Bamby fibreglass three-wheeler in 1983 it had, in reality, little chance of being accepted as a practical form of transport. Had he launched his microcar today it might well have been met with a totally different response.

Ligier and Aixam microcars have their particular position within the market place, and who, a few years ago, would have thought that the Smart would have become a familiar sight on our roads and motorways? Who, too, would have believed that the Reliant Robin is still being manufactured in 2002, and that the Reliant company is excelling in bringing to the United Kingdom the Piaggio range of Ape three-wheel commercials that have been part of Italy's motoring scene for the past fifty years? Electric cars too have their place, and the Corbin Sparrow with styling reminiscent of the original Fend offers clean and economical commuter transport.

The new-generation microcars such as the Ligier Ambra and Aixam 500 Evolution have evolved into relatively complex vehicles. Legislation has meant that these cars have built-in

---

Smart

A design that was conceived by Nicolas Hayek of Smart Watches, the Smart car was built by Daimler-Benz at Hambach in northern France and incorporated into Daimler Chrylser on its establishment. Production began in July 1998 and in 2002 a convertible edition was launched. Right-hand-drive models were available from November 2001. Building the Smart involved some unique processes, such as powder-spray coating the chassis in preference to conventional paint, and use of 85 per cent of materials that are recyclable. Smart has pushed the microcar concept into a whole new aspect of acceptability.

The Corbin Sparrow is a single-seat electric commuter car. Top speed is 65mph (105km/h) with a range of between 40–60 miles (64–100km) per battery charge. (Corbin)

The Smart has achieved a huge success in the short time it has been available. Small, easy to park and having outstanding performance, it has boosted the microcar revival enormously.

The Smart is marketed by Daimler-Chrysler and is available in a range of models. This is the Smart City-Coupé. (Smart)

The Smart is available with either manual or automatic transmission. Six-speed gearboxes are fitted which can be switched from sequential action to fully auto according to model. (Smart)

Smart

Chassis

Type   Integral

Engine (Smart & Pure)

Layout   Petrol; three cylinders in-
                        line, two valves per cylinder
Peak power   44bhp @ 5,250rpm (Smart
                        & Pulse: 61bhp @5,250rpm;
                        Smart & Passion: 54bhp
                        @5,250rpm)
Bore × stroke   63.5 × 63mm
Cubic capacity   599cc
Compression ratio   9.5:1

Transmission

Clutch   Smart & Pure: single dry-
                        plate; Smart & Pulse: single-
                        plate dry disc; Smart &
                        Passion: single-plate dry disc
Gearbox   All: six-speed

Note: With softip shift there is no need for a clutch
when changing gear. Softouch automatic
transmission allows drivers to switch between
manual and automatic mode at the flick of a
selector on the gearshift knob

Brakes (All)

Type   ABS braking with two
                        circuits and servo assistance;
                        front discs, rear drums,
                        electronic braking force
                        distribution

Suspension (All)

Type   New McPherson strut front
                        suspension, stabilizer rod;
                        rear suspension has De Dion
                        axle, coil springs, shock
                        absorbers and stabilizer rod

Steering (All)

Type   Rack and pinion with
                        steering dampers

Wheels & tyres (All)

Wheels   F/r 4J × 15/5.5J × 15
Tyres   F/r 145/65 R15 / 175/55
                        R15

Dimensions (All)

Length   2,500mm (8ft 1½in)
Width   1,515mm (4ft 11in)
Height   1,549mm (5ft ½in)
Wheelbase   1,812mm (5ft 10¾in)
Track   front: 1,116mm (3ft 8in);
                        rear: 1,041mm (3ft 5in)
Weight   1,590lb (720kg)

Performance (All)

Top speed   85mph (137km/h)
Fuel consumption   Urban: 46.3mpg (6ltr/
                        100km); combined cycle:
                        57.6mpg (4.9ltr/100km);
                        extra urban: 65.7mpg
                        (4.3ltr/100km)

Nissan has marketed this cute microvan which, as pictured here, is being used for publicity purposes.

safety technology that accounts for stability and impact testing in the same manner as conventional cars. On modern microcars, diesel engines of around 500cc provide respectable performance together with 70mpg (4ltr/100km) fuel economy. Unseen on microcars of past generations are levels of trim and equipment that include automatic transmission, electric windows and door release, central locking, optional leather trim and more. No more than a few years ago, few luxury saloons could boast such comprehensive features.

A significant development in the microcar revival is an appearance of a prototype Volkswagen that is capable of consuming less than 1ltr of diesel per 100km. The '1-litre' car was first displayed in the spring of 2002 when Dr Ferdinand Piëch drove the car from Wolfsburg to Hamburg at the time of VW's annual general meeting. Fitted with a mid-engined 0.3ltr single-cylinder diesel unit, the car, which weighs only 290kg (640lb), can reach 120km/h (75mph) thanks to a design that is very aerodynamic and which makes use of composite carbon-fibre reinforced metal. When looking at the car one cannot help but think the styling is reminiscent of the Messerschmitt of half a century earlier.

Microcars have evolved into high-performance machines that are designed to offer quality motoring while being economical to run. On today's congested roads they provide an alternative to more conventional cars, and one thing is

This micro pickup was spotted in Versailles when being used for street cleaning purposes.

The interior of the Smart City-Coupé. (Smart)

certain, we will be seeing more of them in the future. Whether they are viewed as being as charismatic as the bubblecars and minicars of previous generations is a matter of personal opinion. Younger motorists experiencing new-generation microcars will undoubtedly derive just as much fun and pleasure as did drivers of early Bonds, Reliants, Isettas, Messerschmitts and that plethora of tiny machines that collectively constituted minimal motoring.

The microcar of the future? This three-wheeled Volkswagen has overtones of the Messerschmitt and can achieve 283mpg (1ltr/100km). (Volkswagen)

Index